This book is dedicated to Shri Sai, my grandfather, my wife, my daughter, and of course, all of you who read it!

INTRODUCTION

Thank you for purchasing the book, and you are now officially part of the DevOps community! If you want to understand DevOps and you are a manager or a DevOps enthusiast, this book is for you. Then you should read this book.

Thousands of books and articles on DevOps teach the various approaches to implement DevOps. Those discussions about ideal procedures and organisational structures. Very few of them, if any, went into detail about things that should avoid. Adopting modern-day DevOps calls for a bottom-up approach to implementing the significant initiative and reverse mentoring. That is a piece of the composition for this book here.

This book discusses the things that organisations should steer clear of as well as the blind spots that they typically overlook in the process of adoption. But with a constructive attitude. To provide businesses and business professionals with the opportunity to view the adoption of DevOps in a way that is fresher and has different lenses! This book is written for businesspeople and other non-technical individuals interested in learning about the DevOps methodology. Because of this, I have attempted to construct the contents without using technical jargon.

Have fun reading!

The DevOps Mokitas

SARAVANAN LAKSHMANAN

Avoid the Elephants in your DevOps Adoption: A Handbook of DevOps mistakes to avoid

AUTOMATION???!!!

WHERE IS THE TESTER ???!!!

Here is what they always forget to tell new testers in the job interview

DEVOPS MEANS TO ME?

RECRUITMENT

HOW TO SPOT A REALLY GOOD TESTER FROM JUST A TESTER

THE DEVOPS MOKITAS

Avoid the Elephants in your DevOps Adoption:

A Handbook of Devops Don'ts to avoid

Saravanan Lakshmanan

CONTENTS

PART 1 – INTRODUCTION

CHAPTER 1: WHAT IS DEVOPS, AND WHAT PROBLEM DOES IT SOLVE? WHY DO YOU NEED THAT? WHY DOES DEVOPS FAILURE HAPPEN?

Devops: Consist of cultural philosophies, practises, and tools that enhance an organisation's ability to deliver applications and services at high speed.

What is DevOps?

DevOps is the union of software development and IT operations. DevOps aims to build and release the codes or features of the software with minimal delays. Then, test that code in a virtual environment before it's deployed to production. Finally, keep IT operations working efficiently by automating processes. In other words, DevOps is about collaboration between developers and IT ops professionals.

DevOps is one of the most talked about trends in software today. Unfortunately, it has also been the cause of confusion and conflicts among those who tend to take a black-and-white approach to things. DevOps is not simply combining two words into one acronym.

Instead, it's a set of principles, procedures and practices that work together to help organisations optimise processes between software developers and IT operations teams. So that new software gets deployed faster with fewer bugs and at lower costs. The benefits of implementing DevOps are numerous: faster time to market, improved collaboration between development & operations, higher feature quality, reduced release cycles and quicker detection of performance issues through monitoring tools.

What Problem does DevOps Solve for you, and What is a successful DevOps implementation?

A successful DevOps implementation is one where everyone has bought into the idea that they will work collaboratively and efficiently to do the following.

Produce high-quality software: Developers and operations teams write code that does what it is supposed to and doesn't have any bugs.

Release software frequently: Teams release software frequently, which means that customers receive new features faster.

Get more value from the existing infrastructure: Companies use existing infrastructure to support new products and services.

Use the same tools and technology: All teams use the same tools and technology. Practicing this makes it easier for everyone to share information and collaborate.

Why is there so much debate around DevOps?

There is much debate around DevOps because it is an inclusive term with no universal definition. There is no standard way to implement it, so there needs to be more clarity. Some organisations might implement continuous delivery, a subset of DevOps. Others might implement Agile or focus on continuous integration, another subset of DevOps. - Other organisations might be implementing Lean, a separate concept from DevOps. In some organisations, DevOps is an office that does the work of all three of the above. In contrast, a team is responsible for each of these activities in others.

Why do you need DevOps?

Businesses thrive on innovation and creativity, and so does software development. So it's crucial to promote a culture of change and experimentation. This way, you can be sure your company will remain agile and able to respond to the ever-changing demands of the marketplace. If you want your organisation to succeed in today's market, you must have an agile and flexible organisation.

You must be able to make changes quickly and deploy new software daily. And deliver customer value quickly and can pivot when needed. And you must be able to change your focus when needed to address a significant new challenge or opportunity. And, of course, you must have a high-performing team.

DevOps failure reasons

If you're going to succeed in DevOps, you must first identify the reasons why organisations fail at DevOps. As you know, this is challenging as every organisation has different goals and may be at different stages of its DevOps journey. Therefore, what fails one organisation might not be the same as failing another. However, the following are a few factors that could cause a DevOps failure.

Poor communication: Since DevOps is a culture shift, the entire organisation must know what it means and how everyone can benefit from it. An organisation with a poor communication culture will have difficulty adopting a DevOps mentality.

Lack of ownership: When you have a siloed organisation, it's easier to execute on DevOps because there needs to be clear ownership. One department is responsible for writing code, while another is responsible for testing it. If a feature has a problem in production, there's no clear owner accountable for fixing it.

Lack of visibility: One of the biggest challenges will be more visibility between development and operations teams. It means you must learn how your code works or what's happening with your infrastructure. As a result, operations teams could be affected by the code releases or feel overwhelmed by the new tasks DevOps requires

Infrastructure issues: If organisations address the problems that often arise with legacy, non-cloud-capable, on-premise infrastructure, they'll be able to adopt DevOps.

Key reasons why Organisations fail in DevOps:

The fact is that DevOps is a cultural shift and not simply a process change. The truth is that many organisations need the right tech and talent to implement DevOps. So let us look at other Key strings of the reason for the failures.

Poor culture fit: One of the biggest reasons organisations fail at DevOps. Suppose you hire people who are not a cultural fit. In that case, they are unlikely to succeed no matter how much you try to modify their behaviours. So, in the early stages of adopting DevOps, you must make hiring decisions based on cultural fit. Hire people who are flexible, open-minded, and collaborative.

Poor planning: If you fail to plan, you are planning to fail. It would be best if you had a clear plan for implementing DevOps and a strategy for how you will get there. Start with a pilot project or proof of concept where you can test ideas and see what works.

Using the right tools: You must use the right tools and technology to implement DevOps. It's vital that you find the right tool for each problem and that you use them consistently. It's also essential that your tools are compatible and integrated with the other tools in your ecosystem.

You need to understand the cultural transformation required: You need to understand the cultural shift required to have difficulty implementing DevOps. You must look at your current organisation and culture and see what needs to change.

A few other reasons and causes for the DevOps Transformation failures are listed below.

1. Organisational silos and a lack of ownership.
2. Failing to hire the right people for DevOps and hiring for cultural fit rather than skill.
3. Need to understand and/or design for the necessary cultural transformation.
4. Using outdated tools and practices.
5. Need to measure and track the right metrics to see if it's working.
6. Need a plan and a strategy for implementing DevOps.

In a Nutshell, the best way to ensure you don't experience a DevOps failure is to provide you with an understanding of what it is, what it means and how to implement it successfully. If you know what to look out for, you can better manage the risks associated with this trend and avoid the pitfalls that could lead to failure. And with some luck, you can avoid the confusion and debate around this topic.

PART 2 – MOKITAS IN THE CULTURE ROOM

CHAPTER 1: UNDERSTANDING THE CORE VALUES OF DEVOPS

- **Core Values:** Characteristics or attributes that are not only admirable but also reflect the highest objectives, cherished convictions, and underlying influencing factors of an individual or an organisation

What are DevOps Goals, and why do we need to understand them? Good Question, right? Let me tell you; that the primary reason for DevOps Transformation failure.

While the organisation embarks on this Journey, they expect that DevOps will do plenty of things and fail to establish the goals, visions, and roadmaps and most of the Stakeholders' points of view.

1. DevOps is a collection of Tool Chain
2. DevOps is Automation
3. DevOps is Process Governance
4. DevOps is Collaboration
5. DevOps is Agile

In reality, it's more than above all points the points listed. So, let's take a wholesale look at the Goals and Cultural Framework of DevOps.

What are DevOps Goals?

The goal of DevOps is to establish streamlined just-in-time business processes. DevOps aims to maximise business outcomes by increasing sales and profitability, enhancing business speed, or minimising operating costs by aligning just-in-time processes. DevOps establish the IT service supply chain in the business as the supply chain for other products is embedded within the organisation's business.

It is a significant paradigm shift from software delivery to providing IT services. Therefore, DevOps needs to establish an automated quick-deployment system from an architectural perspective.

There are many methods and tools available. However, DevOps doesn't have a template for implementation. Every organisation needs to think and build its own DevOps Business improvement process. Therefore, it is essential to understand the DevOps concept to run the process efficiently according to the appropriate procedure. Let's Take a Look at the Goals. The generally accepted goal in the DevOps world is CALMS, Actually, CALMS is a framework. The Ultimate goal would be achieving the framework.

But this book is slightly different from that CALMS; S stands for sharing, but we stress that as Sharing/sustain.

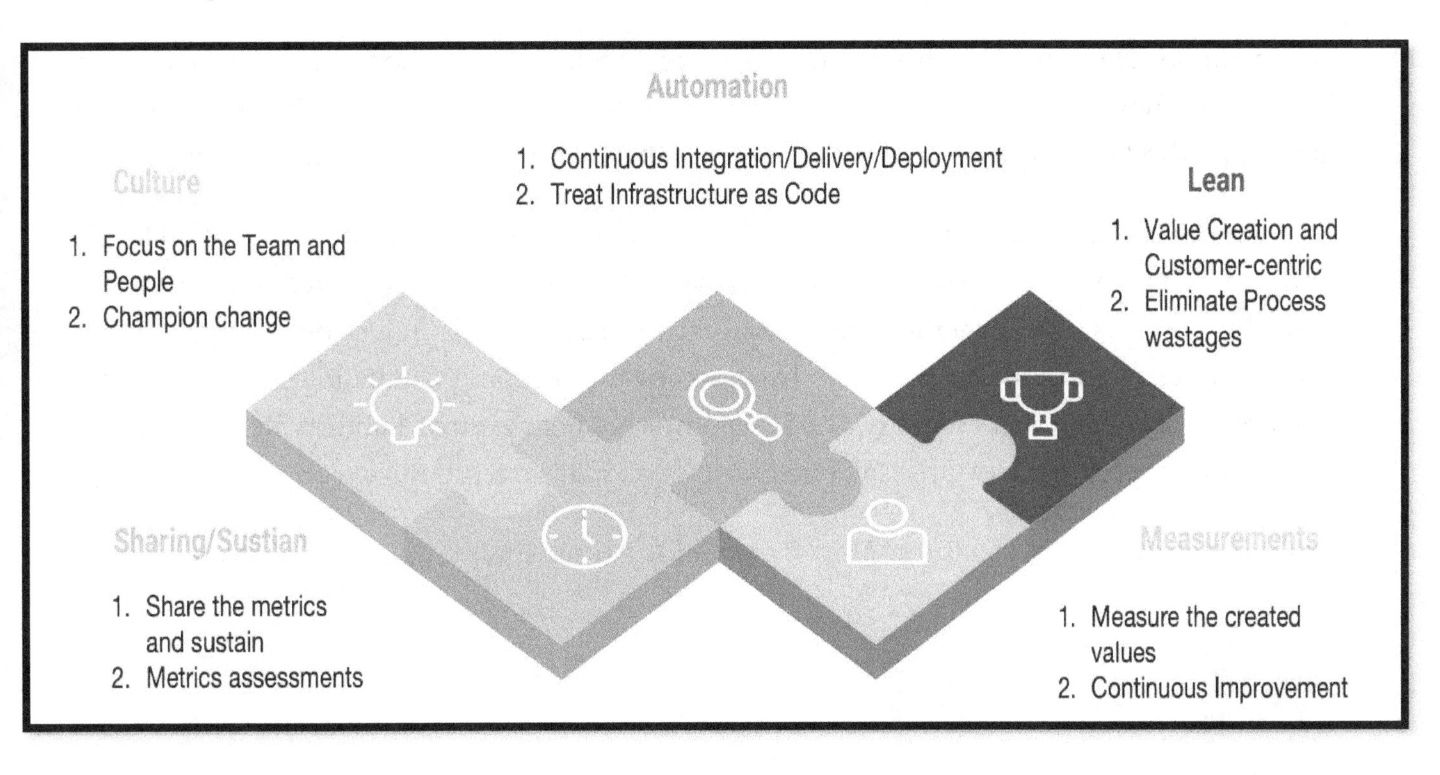

DevOps is an evolution of the operations team's agile teams. Also, organisations thinking about DevOps Transformation better consider Agile as a combo. As Agile and DevOps Work together well, product-oriented teams allow for a smoother product development process with team members more focused on what they need to do.

When building a DevOps Culture, it is highly suggested to include every team based on the Blast Radius exercise. Such as development, QA, product management, design, operations, project management, Business Stakeholders, IT Securities, Process governance, and any other skill set long-running product requires to meet Customer requirements. Hiring DevOps professionals and rebranding existing resources or teams into DevOps teams without prior or adequate training is not advisable.

For IT Service companies Can, Add ITIL Framework with Agile methodologies will yield maximum benefits while manufacturing companies like Toyota are adopting the Andon cord and Kata model.

Few things can foster collaboration as well as commonly shared goals. As a result, some companies have switched to product-based teams and found it too much too soon, which eventually ended as a failure model.

For example, Dev and Ops teams should work together to develop solutions. They can integrate by having Dev team members join Ops meetings and vice versa. It's a nimble and natural method for getting on the beat of one another's work, thoughts, and conflicts.

The best organisations are energetic about DevOps culture across each office and at all levels of the organisation graph. The expression "DevOps" is frequently too limited at a vast scale, and the term is not generally required. Such organisations have open channels of correspondence and talk consistently. They accept that keeping clients blissful is the same amount of item the board's liability as it is the improvement group's liability. Remember that They comprehend that DevOps isn't one group's work. It's everybody's work.

Understand more about Culture? Now it's time for Automation.

Automation

Even a no-brainer can enunciate that Using Automation can save people time and effort and make it much easier to manage the business. It also ensures a consistent workflow.

Building, testing, deploying, and provisioning automation is an excellent place to start for any team that isn't already doing them. Working together on these things benefits all team members with new tools for their jobs. In addition, it encourages cross-working that helps all company departments.

Automation usually starts with continuous delivery: running each code change through a gauntlet of automated tests, often facilitated by On-premises or cloud-based infrastructure. The DevOps team then packages up builds and promotes them through environments using continuous deployments thru Automation.

Systems are executed more rigorously through Test Automation Suites. These tests quickly catch bugs and security flaws, and automated deployments alert IT/Ops about drift between environments, reducing surprises at release time.

DevOps is not just about getting your code from one place to another; it's about ensuring that your system's configuration can be easily managed and distributed. When developers write modular and composable codes with configurable parts, they create a more reliable and maintainable system.

"Continuous Integration" and "continuous delivery" are two of the most robust concepts in the DevOps world. However, other types of Automation exist. Nevertheless, they're worth mentioning because they help break down the wall between development and operations. And when DevOps uses automated deploys to send thoroughly tested code to identically supplied environments.

Well! Now we have an idea of Automation. What's next? Hm... Let's lean on Lean.

Lean

You may have heard theory if you're into software development. It's a balance. It's a balance between being fast, steady, and scrappy. When it comes to DevOps-related terminology like continuous improvement and embracing change, these core concepts are also an integral part of lean.

A DevOps mindset is all about continuous improvement and always keeping an eye out for new opportunities. Some are more obvious, like retrospectives with your team to improve your processes, while others are slightly more subtle. For example, A/B testing new on-boardings can help understand how to make onboarding easier for users.

It's thanks to agile development that continuous improvement is now considered mainstream.

One key tenant of the agile methodology is to get products into customers' hands as soon as possible. A 'perfect' product six months from now is only worth a little if customers' needs change or the competition offers a better solution. Customers are more likely to stay with a company that continues to improve its favourite features.

The DevOps aspiring organisation should prepare teams to progress despite failures because they are unavoidable. Keep an eye on 'anti-fragility'; this is designed for when something goes wrong.

In a DevOps-driven environment, failure isn't penalised. Teams are aware that things can go wrong, so they plan extensively. They realise that fast detection and quick recovery are at the core of a thriving production environment.

Post-mortems are all about looking at where things have fallen and working on improving them. Mistakes can happen to anyone, and the objective of a post-mortem analysis is to bring up ideas of how to fix these, so it does not happen again.

Suitable pieces of stuff! Let's jump to our following essential Goals and Core value Subject. It's Measurements and metrics! It sounds scary or exciting? Let's take a deep dive to get a clear understanding of metrics.

Measurements

Performance indicators make it easier to ascertain whether your continuous improvement initiatives are successful. Fortunately, you can keep track of a multitude of performance metrics with various technologies and tools, such as the number of time users spend on your site, whether a blog post produced any sales, or how frequently critical alerts appear in your logs. However, you can measure only some things. When you first begin, focus on the fundamentals:

1. How long does it take to go from development to deployment?
2. What are the error rates and repeat errors that occur?
3. How long does it take to recover from a system crash?
4. What is the current number of users?
5. How many users gained or lost in the current week?
6. What is the Cycle time?
7. What is the Deployment frequency?

A solid foundation enables you to collect more sophisticated metrics around feature usage, customer journeys, and service level agreements (SLAs). This information comes in handy when it is time for the road map and new features of the product.

Your team can use all this succulent data to make decisions, but it's even more effective when shared with other teams—especially those in other departments. Your Product group, for example, wants to build new features, but Product owners are concerned about customer churn due to the product's high technical debt. By providing valuable data that supports your roadmap, even if it has fewer features and more corrections, you can build consensus and gain support from stakeholders.

Sharing/Sustaining

We wanted it to be possible for one simple 'magic wand' to turn all businesses into high-performing DevOps teams, but DevOps transformations require different practices and philosophies. With the help of DevOps tools, you could become a top-performing DevOps team. They will simplify, enhance, and speed up your workflow, help you organise processes, and lead to success. Despite this, breaking down Development and Operations siloes has several positive effects on business. They include better trust, faster software releases, more reliable deployments, and a better team feedback loop.

It's evident that Embracing DevOps comes with many challenges, but adopting the right mindset and making the necessary effort can also lead to significant benefits.

There has always been friction between the development and operations teams, but we must overcome this divide by sharing responsibilities. Success goes a long way in repairing this divide.

Developers can win instant goodwill by helping to carry one of the operations' most enormous burdens: the Developers (a figurative construct these days). DevOps is big on the idea that the same people who build an application should be involved in Build and support, so can you help with these processes?

In a Nutshell, out of this concept comes the phrase "Build and Run", which fosters a hands-on approach across teams. It doesn't mean you need to hire developers and quickly expect them to be excellent operators. Instead, developers and operators pair with one another throughout the application's lifecycle. Moreover, reports have shown that peer-reviewed code and products are the sole reviews that result in excellent delivery and performance; in fact, external reviewers were no more straightforward than conducting no review.

Teams that embrace DevOps will have rotating roles and responsibilities whereby developers address issues encountered by end users while troubleshooting production problems simultaneously. This person responds to urgent customer-reported issues, creates patches when necessary, and works through the backlog of customer-reported defects. As a result, the "developer on support" learns plenty about how the application functions in the wild. And by being highly available to the operations team, the event teams build trust and mutual respect.

Suppose you still need to receive the goals. Then, your organisation may have lots of Impacts not limited to

Operational complexity: DevOps creates new operational complexities by breaking down the silos between development and operations teams. The teams may need help understanding each other because they need to get used to talking and having their language. This will lead to new operational complexities like managing team interdependencies and conflicting priorities.

CHAPTER 2: SETTING UP A CULTURE

- **Culture:** Collectively, the arts and other examples of human intellectual achievement.

Now, you are aware of What DevOps culture is. The question is how to transform Your Organisation into a DevOps Culture. What are all the critical factors involved in it? Curious?... Let's jump, then!

DevOps is the combination of technologies, processes, and mindsets that come together to drive digital organisations. A culture of continuous learning, collaboration, and trust are critical to the success of a DevOps implementation. However, establishing a culture of DevOps and moving an organisation to become a DevOps organisation can be challenging. In this Chapter, let us explore how you can transform your organisation into a DevOps culture and gain operational excellence through the principles of DevOps. Let's dive in!

A DevOps culture is the set of values, beliefs, and attitudes that make up how people work together in an organisation. It is the environment, or the context, in which people operate and make decisions. When DevOps is working well, it is invisible; people take it for granted as the way things are done. But the culture is broken when an organisation needs to deliver the right products to customers correctly. So, to transform the organisation into a DevOps organisation, you must first understand the organisational culture.

Defining your organisational culture

What is Organisational Behavior? Organisational behaviour is the study of social interactions and relationships within organisations. Behavioural studies focus on how individuals in the organisation make decisions, why they make those decisions, and how those decisions impact the organisation. Organisational culture is a powerful force shaping how people work and interact. The shared values, beliefs, and assumptions guide decision-making and actions across the organisation. It is the unwritten rulebook for how things get done.

Culture is the bond that holds an organisation together. When times are good and the glue that keeps people together when the going gets tough.

What is Organizational Climate? Organisational climate refers to the emotional and perceptual aspects of the workplace environment. It includes how people feel about their jobs, their co-workers, the leadership in place, and the company's goals. Climate is determined by a combination of employees' perceptions of their work environment and their emotional reactions to those perceptions. Climate is the mood or feeling that surrounds the work environment. It is more subjective than culture and is often measured using surveys.

Create Organisational Awareness

Organisational awareness is the first step toward transforming your organisation into a DevOps culture. It is the process of understanding and adopting the organisational culture and identifying the gaps in the current state. Organisations must go through a series of stages while becoming more aware of a culture: awareness, observation, and insight. To create awareness within your organisation, you can use a wide variety of strategies: Such as

Organisational surveys: Surveys are a great way to collect data and gain insight into the current state of your organisation. You can use many surveys to collect data on your organisation's culture and everything.

Organisational walkthroughs are a great way to help you understand your organisation. It allows you to walk around the organisation and talk to people on all levels of the org chart.

Organisational journaling: Journaling is an excellent way for the management team to gain insight into the organisation's current state. It helps you look inside the organisation and understand how different departments work together.

Establishing the principles of a DevOps Culture

Once you better understand the organisational culture, you can identify the gaps and opportunities for improvement. Then, you can start initiating cultural changes by adopting DevOps principles. Each of these principles aims to create a more effective, efficient, and sustainable culture across the organisation. These principles are not mutually exclusive and are meant to be combined.

Focus on People: DevOps is built on trust and respect. When people feel valued and recognised, they see their work as more than just their job — they feel like they are a part of something bigger than themselves. This sense of belonging and ownership is critical to achieving high performance, high satisfaction, and low turnover.

Focus on Purpose: All organisations exist to solve problems. A clear understanding of why your organisation exists and what problems it is trying to solve will empower people to find creative and innovative ways to achieve the mission.

Focus on Delivery: Successful enterprises ship value and solve problems for customers. They focus on continuous delivery of all product types and end-to-end service delivery.

Focus on Culture: Transformational change comes from the inside out. So, to transform your organisation, you must start with culture. Fortunately, DevOps is constructed on a set of principles that are ideal for changing culture.

Proactive Culture

Continuously Inspect and Adapt the best way to achieve a high-performing culture and operational excellence is to continuously inspect and adapt your organisation. In the DevOps world, this is called Cultural Transformation. Cultural transformation is an organisation-wide effort to change behaviours and improve the culture. Therefore, you need a consistent and reliable process for continuous inspection and cultural transformation.

There are various ways to implement an organisational culture change process.

Cultural Change Board: A cultural change board is a team responsible for driving cultural change across the organisation. It is a great way to create consistent work across the entire organisation and drive organisational change.

Cultural Change Scorecard: A cultural change scorecard helps you measure how well your organisation is doing. It gives you a clear view of what needs to be changed and how to improve the culture.

Cultural Change Agile Board: An agile board is a great way to help you with cultural change. It allows you to work on continuous improvement and achieve goals.

Combined Culture

Together, Always Be Shipping

A collaborative organisation fosters collaboration across functional groups, teams, and individuals. It shows that stakeholders are working together to achieve common goals and working in an interdependent manner to produce an end-to-end flow of value. A collaborative culture is critical to achieving continuous delivery across the organisation. It is essential always to be shipping and to be producing something consistently. At the Centre of a collaborative culture is the need for transparency. To create a culture of openness, you must find ways to make information accessible to all organisational stakeholders.

Here are some ways to make your organisation more transparent:

Create a culture of sharing: Create a culture where people constantly share their knowledge and expertise with others across the organisation. This will help to cultivate a sense of collaboration across the organisation.

Build a culture of feedback: Create a culture where people feel comfortable giving feedback to one another. When you create a culture of feedback, you help people improve their skills and make them feel more comfortable with sharing their ideas.

Create a transparent culture where people know what is happening across the entire organisation. Make sure that people understand how their work fits into the bigger picture.

Trust-based Culture: Be Responsible for Everything

A trust-based culture is one in which people feel comfortable admitting their mistakes. Feel confident that others will help them solve problems and feel empowered to take on new challenges.

A trust-based culture is one where people are responsible for everything that happens in the organisation. There are a few ways to foster a trust-based culture within your organisation:

Create an environment where it's safe to fail: In a trust-based culture, it's crucial to create an environment where it's safe to fall. Doing so conveys that people will feel comfortable admitting when they make mistakes, even if it's something that could have been avoided.

Enable people to take responsibility for their work. In a trust-based culture, people must be empowered to take responsibility for their work. They need to know that their work has meaning and matters.

Foster a sense of consistency and urgency across the organisation: Within a trust-based culture, consistency is key. Everyone needs to be doing the same things, and they need to be doing them in the same way. This will help foster trust across the organisation.

Changing the organisational culture to become a DevOps organisation

Now that you understand what a DevOps culture is and how you can implement it within

CHAPTER 3: AVOIDING TEAM TOPOLOGIES

- **Team topologies:** A collection of those other team types that provide a compelling product to accelerate delivery by Stream-aligned teams.

As you know, DevOps has many principles and practices that help to facilitate communication, collaboration, and continuous feedback between software developers and information technology (IT) departments. However, when implementing new DevOps strategies in your organisation, you need the right people to help you succeed. To accomplish that, you need a transformation plan. Therefore, it's best to assemble a team of individuals well-versed in DevOps principles and techniques. However, finding the right people can take time and effort, especially if you need help finding where to look. To make things slightly more manageable for you. Let me suggest an overview of several different DevOps team topologies that can be useful when setting up your transformation team. Read on to learn more about these topologies and which might be best for your organisation.

What is a DevOps team?

At its core, DevOps is a culture and a set of practices designed to help accelerate the flow of software development. However, no two DevOps teams are exactly alike. Because every organisation is different, there's no such thing as a "standard" DevOps team. Instead, each DevOps team is unique and custom-tailored to the organisation in which it operates.

In this Chapter, we'll walk you through several team topologies commonly used in DevOps transformations. By reading through this Chapter, you'll learn about each topology and discover which might be best for your organisation. Let's get started!

The Culture Shaping Squad

The culture-shaping team is responsible for building the DevOps culture in an organisation. This team usually consists of executives and senior-level managers committed to mentoring, coaching, and supporting fellow employees. This team is critical during the early stages of transformation because they're responsible for setting the tone and creating an environment where DevOps can flourish. For example, suppose a manager or executive is only partially on board with your transformation plan. In that case, it can negatively impact the growth of your team. So, a culture-shaping squad is much more critical.

The Lean Change Agent Squad

The Lean change agent Squad is responsible for facilitating change across an organisation. This Squad should include individuals who are well-versed in the change management approach and are capable of leading change initiatives throughout the company. The change agent team is often found in organisations already experiencing some transformation. In these environments, the lean change agent squad is tasked with helping to facilitate change to the DevOps transformation itself.

The Automation Expert Squad

The automation expert team is responsible for designing, building, and implementing continuous improvement initiatives. This Squad typically includes individuals who excel at designing and building automated systems and software tools. The automation expert team is responsible for designing, building, and implementing continuous improvement initiatives.

This group is critical during the execution phase of your transformation as they're responsible for implementing and managing the tools and techniques that will facilitate the growth and success of your company.

The Continuous Improvement Squad

The continuous improvement Squad is responsible for implementing improvement initiatives across an organisation. This crew usually includes employees with a background in quality assurance, testing, or engineering.

The continuous improvement squad is essential during the execution phase of your transformation. Because this unit is responsible for implementing the tools and processes that will help facilitate continuous improvement across your organisation.

A CI/CD Tester and Quality Analyst Squad

The CI/CD tester and quality analyst team is responsible for facilitating and executing quality activities throughout an organisation. This team usually includes quality assurance engineers, testers, and analysts responsible for validating and verifying that a product or service is operating as expected.

The CI/CD tester and quality analyst team are critical during your transformation's execution phase. They are responsible for implementing the tools and processes to help facilitate quality activities across your organisation.

An Infrastructure as Code Squad

The infrastructure as code bloc is responsible for managing and implementing an automation strategy that facilitates infrastructure as code. This team usually includes engineers with a background in software development or application architecture.

The infrastructure as code team is critical during the execution phase of your transformation as they are responsible for managing, monitoring, and implementing an automation strategy that facilitates infrastructure as code.

A Developer and Automation Engineer Squad

The developer and automation engineer team are responsible for designing and building the tools and software that facilitate the CI/CD process. This team usually includes engineers with a background in software development or application architecture.

The developer and automation engineer team are critical during the execution phase of your transformation. They are responsible for designing and building the tools and software that facilitate the CI/CD process.

Site Reliability Engineering Squad

The site reliability engineering team is a team that works on software applications and systems throughout the organisation. Their focus is to ensure the company's IT infrastructure is always available, secure, and scalable. They check for new bugs in code or configuration changes that could affect the application's stability, performance, security, or scalability. They also ensure other teams have access to resources when needed to build their applications or systems as expected.

The Site Reliability Engineering team is critical during your transformation's execution phase. They are responsible for Site Reliability and System uptime.

In a Nutshell, as you can see, DevOps transformations can be challenging. Because there are many moving parts, you must ensure that everything comes together at the right time. It could be difficult for organisations that need the right people on board. However, your transformation will go much smoother with the right team topologies.

CHAPTER 4: AVOIDING A DEVOPS COACH

- **DevOps Coach:** A person who enables and sustains the DevOps transformation.

DevOps is a methodology that helps streamline software processes. It brings together developers and operations teams to work more efficiently by sharing knowledge, best practices, and tools. Suppose you want to implement DevOps at your company but need help figuring out how to get started. In that case, a DevOps coach can help accelerate your efforts. A coach can also provide insight from an outside perspective and see things differently. With their assistance, you can get the most out of your DevOps initiative sooner rather than later.

What Is a DevOps Coach?

DevOps Coach and DevOps consultants get tossed around a lot, and sometimes it takes effort to know exactly what each role involves. So, if you're unfamiliar with these concepts and are wondering what a DevOps coach does, let's start there. A DevOps coach is a facilitator who helps you implement DevOps at your company. This executive-level role focuses on helping strategy, process, and teams become more efficient and effective.

If you're wondering why, you need one, there are a few different reasons:

1. Establishing a DevOps initiative often involves organisational changes. The coach can help the team to work through these organisational changes more smoothly and with less resistance.
2. The coach can help you to define your objectives and select the right tools and processes to meet your goals.

3. They can help you implement the tools and strategies to ensure everything works.

Why You Need a DevOps Coach

As mentioned, a DevOps coach can help you to implement DevOps at your company. This change to your processes or organisation can be disruptive, so having the coach work with your team can help to smooth the transition. The coach can help your team navigate the change, implement the new processes, and get set up with the necessary tools. A Coach can help facilitate a smoother transition and reduce resistance from team members. Another reason you should hire a DevOps coach is to get an outside perspective. If your team has worked closely together for a long time, they may have become too close-minded or close-sighted. They may not look at things from various angles and see new solutions.

A DevOps coach can bring a new perspective, which can help your team identify new solutions and make better decisions when implementing DevOps at your company.

Why Should You Hire a DevOps Coach?

If you want to use DevOps to drive efficiencies and improve how your team works together, there are a few reasons you should hire a coach:

1. The coach can help you plan and organise your DevOps initiative and ensure you get the most out of your efforts.
2. The coach can help you to develop your team and bring everyone up to speed on the new processes and tools they'll be using. This strategy can help your team to operate more efficiently from the start.
3. The coach can help identify and solve any issues during the implementation process.

It will significantly help get the initiative off to a smooth start and ensure the team gets the most out of the effort. Well, had you read enough about the importance of DevOps Coach? Okay, now the question is

How to Find the Right Coach for Your Company?

So, now that you know why a DevOps coach can help your company and why you should hire one, let's talk about how to find the right coach for your Business. To do this, you will need to put together a hiring committee. This committee will consist of Business members involved in the DevOps initiative. You will also want to include members of the IT team who will be using the tools and processes. First, decide how much money you will spend on the coaching effort. Then, put together a hiring committee to find a coach.

The Three Steps Strategies to Finding the Right Coaching fit for your Business

Create a hiring committee: As we mentioned, this committee should consist of Business and IT team members. You can also consider including operations team members, who will need to be involved in the implementation process.

Define the responsibilities of the coaching effort: Make sure everyone is on the same page regarding what the coach will be doing, the time frame they'll be working within, and the budget they'll be working with.

Set up interviews with potential coaches: During these interviews, you can ask the candidates questions to help you decide which coaching fits your Business. You can also tell them about your organisation and the initiative so they can prepare for the interview.

In a Nutshell, hiring a DevOps coach can be a great way to implement DevOps at your company. With the coach's help, you can smooth the transition and reduce the resistance from team members. Once you've hired a coach, you can focus on implementing the new processes and bringing the team up to speed on the tools and technologies they'll need. Beyond that, you'll be able to focus on making your Business more efficient and profitable.

CHAPTER 5: LEVERAGE AGILE TEAM CULTURE

- **Agile:** The ability to both create and respond to change.

Well, from the previous two chapters, you have understood DevOps Topologies, the importance of a DevOps Coach, and how to get one for your transformation Journey. Isn't enough? If you say yes, then you are trapped!

As you know, that DevOps alone cannot do wonders in your organisation. If DevOps is your Train, then you need to have the track to run it! which is where Agile is coming into the ground. Let us see about various Agile Squads and how they work!

Unfortunately, some organisations fail to leverage the Agile Team culture, which affects team cohesiveness, causes misunderstandings about roles and responsibilities, and causes Duties segregation.

Please remember that Agile is empirical. I have suggested the models below from my best experience. So, let's dive deeply into The Ultimate Guide to a Successful Agile Team Organisation: Squads, Chapters, Tribes, and Guilds.

What is an Agile Team?

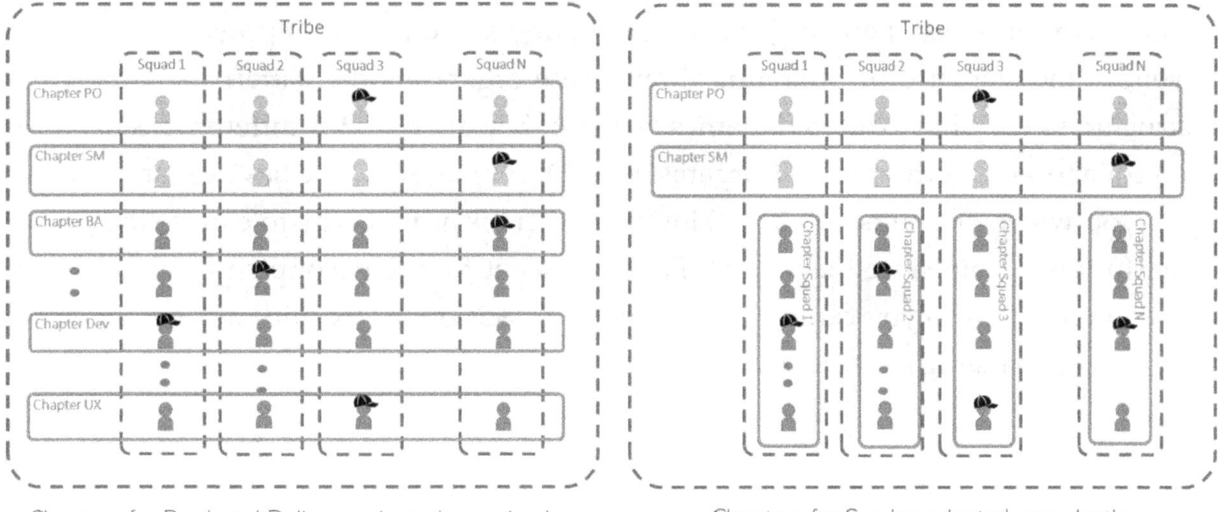

Source: Agile Beyond Boundary

An Agile team is a set of employees, freelancers, or contractors who work on an Agile project. Agile teams are co-located sometimes, and they're entirely dedicated to the project while it lasts. As a result, they don't have to care about any other projects. When creating the product or service, every team member is required. Cross-functional roles are shared, meaning that roles vary depending on the project's requirements and the kind of Agile framework selected.

For example, a Scrum team requires a Scrum master, a product owner, and additional group members. The Scrum master oversees the project, unites the group, and organises daily meetings. The product owner ensures that the product satisfies the customer's demands. A product expert and other stakeholders may participate in the project. However, they are not typically considered part of the Agile team.

Agile teams need to function effectively to deliver timely and cost-effective high-quality software. Therefore, many companies are exploring new ways to structure their agile teams. With the help of these new organisational patterns, you can improve your team's effectiveness and standard of communication. These organisational patterns are known as team structures. They have different names because they are built for different needs: some focus on collaboration, others on self-organisation. Of course, everyone has pros and cons, so it's up to you which one suits you best. However, there is a right way to choose the proper structure for your team since they are all flawed (except for the decoupled form). Here we explain them in detail so you can make an informed decision before adding a new member to your team or changing its structure again.

Squads

A squad is a team of people who work closely together on a specific project. The squad is the smallest unit of an agile team responsible for the project's objectives. Unlike the larger team, which comprises several squads, the squad members do not simultaneously work on any other projects; they are responsible for their assigned tasks. A squad can be between 2 and 6 people accountable for a specific business area.

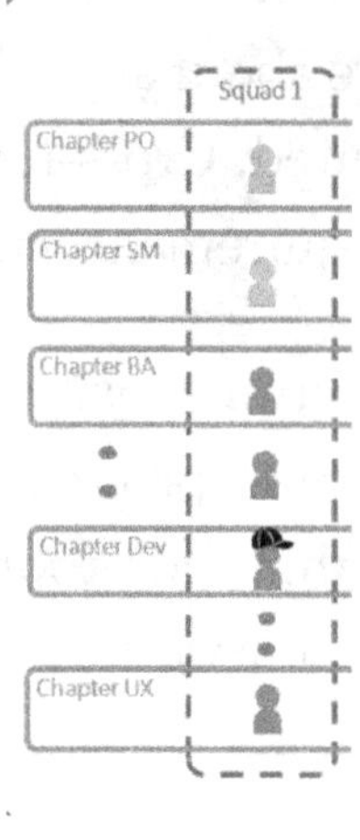

For example, a financial application can have a squad responsible for auditing. In contrast, an external-facing product can have another squad accountable for customer support. Each squad has a leader, who is responsible for the squad's objectives, and a peer-review system to facilitate communication in the team. This team structure is ideal for projects with a specific goal. It needs a smaller number of people working closely together on a particular project.

Chapters

A chapter is a smaller agile team within an organisation. This chapter aims to help groups that are more advanced and less senior to the organisation structure as agile teams. In addition, chapters can create to help individuals or teams who are new to Agile or who need to learn the ropes of Agile.

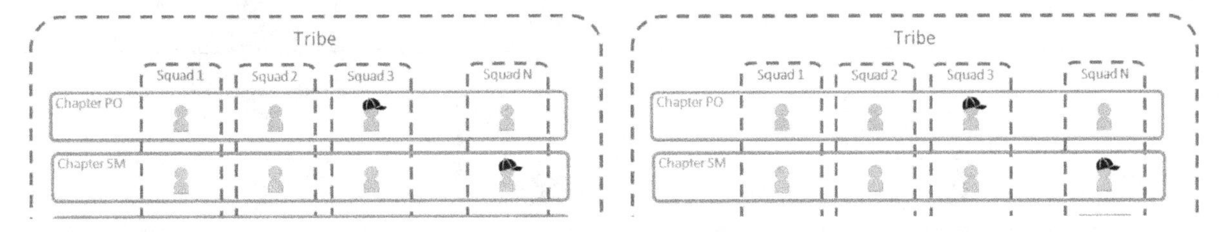

A chapter is a group of people responsible for the same project as their leader and peer-review system. Like a squad, the leader of a chapter is the person responsible for the chapter's objectives. Chapter leaders should be senior to their team members and lead a team of people who can help mentor the members. This can be done through peer reviews, mentoring, or formal training.

Tribes

A tribe is a tribe of teams within an organisation. The purpose of a tribe is to help teams at different levels of experience and/or maturity to co-create and co-organise their work. A tribe of teams is a group of people from other teams who meet regularly to discuss challenges and challenges, share knowledge, and work together. The leader of a tribe is responsible for the tribe's objectives and should be a member of multiple tribes. The tribe leader's role is to facilitate knowledge sharing across teams so that their members can benefit from the expertise of others.

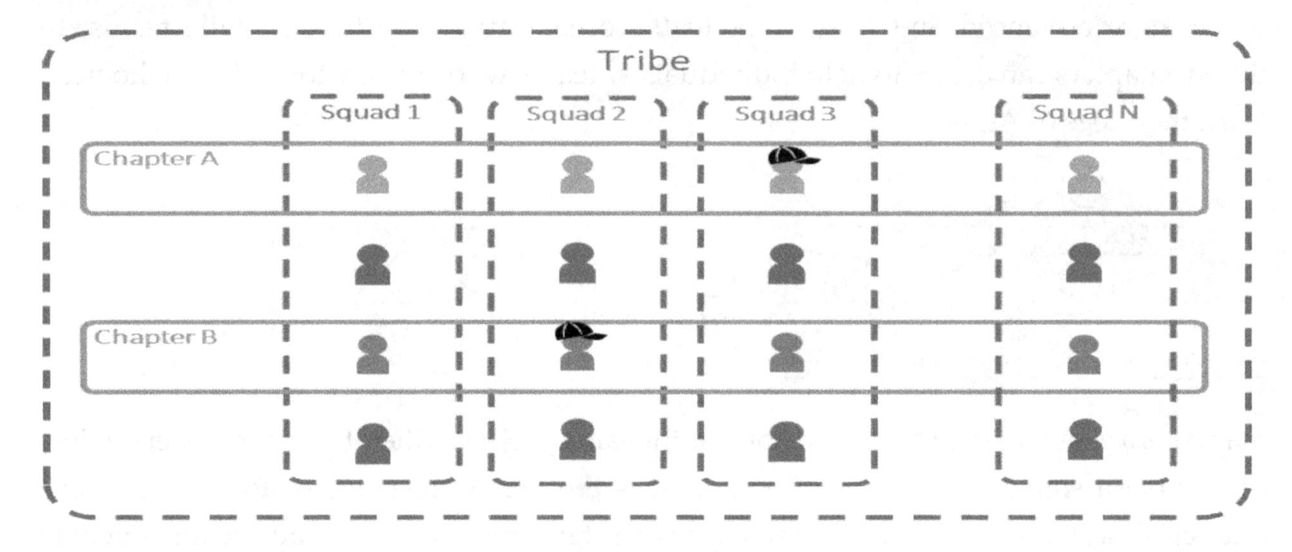

Source: Agile Beyond Boundary

Guild

A guild is a collaboration between teams within an organisation and outside organisations that have a common purpose. A guild of organisations has members with a common interest, such as a topic or a market. An example of a guild could be a collaboration between a team working on financial products and an outside consulting organisation collaborating on a common challenge. The purpose of a guild is to harness the expertise of multiple organisations that work on a common challenge and want to work together to solve that challenge.

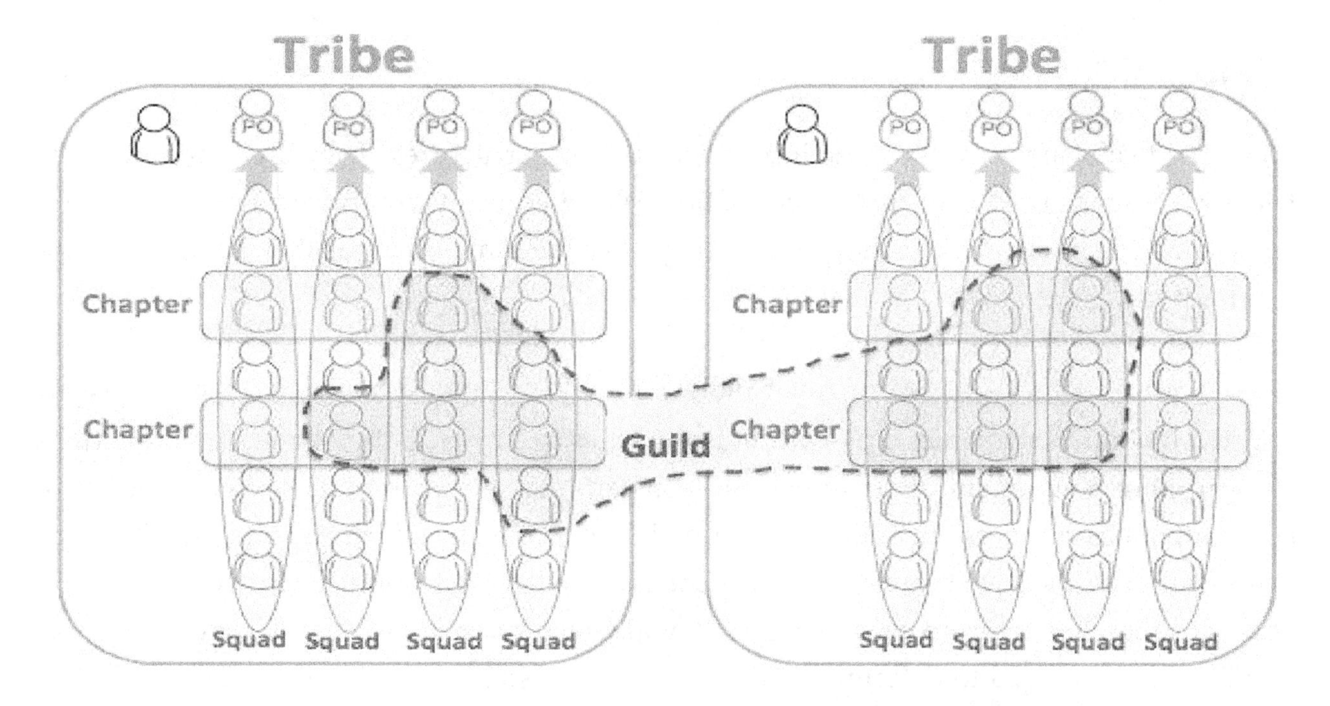

Source: Agility101

Decoupled Teams

A decoupled team is a team that works with other groups outside an organisation that have a common purpose. A decoupled tribe is a tribe of teams outside an organisation with a common goal. A decoupled guild comprises organisations with a common goal outside an organisation. A common goal defines what the teams want to achieve and what benefits they gain from collaborating. In each case, the purpose of a decoupled team, tribe, or guild is to create value among organisations that have a common goal. A decoupled tribe, guild, or team can have members from multiple organisations.

Wrapped Teams

Wrapped teams are a way to combine squad and tribe structures. They are a hybrid of the tribes and squads used in an agile organisation. Wrapped teams comprise members of a tribe and a squad working on the same project. They have the same leader as their squad and tribe counterparts.

In a Nutshell, Agile teams must deliver timely, cost-effective, high-quality software effectively. Many companies are exploring new ways to structure their agile teams. With the help of these new organisational patterns, you can improve your team's effectiveness and standard of communication. There are four main types of team structures: Squads, Chapters, Tribes, and Guilds. Each structure has its benefits and can work for different kinds of teams. Each structure has pros and cons, so it's up to you which suits you best. As an agile coach and team leader, you need to determine what type of team structure your team needs based on their experience and maturity level.

CHAPTER 6: IGNORING THE FRAMEWORK AND METHODOLOGIES

- **Framework:** A foundational structure underlying a system, concept, or idea.
- **Methodology:** A discipline's set of methods, rules, and postulates.

Even a no-brainer can vouch that Software development is a complex process. Numerous challenges and pitfalls exist in any software development process. Hence, it keeps evolving, from the first principles of writing code to the final user-ready product. There is no one perfect way to develop software, but there are practices that can help make your efforts more efficient and effective. A software development framework or methodology is a set of standard rules and principles that guide software development. Depending on the size of your team and the scope of your project, you may find one framework or methodology more beneficial than another. This chapter will enlighten you on the importance of frameworks and methodologies for software development: what is the difference between a framework and methodologies?

These terms are interchangeable, but they have very different meanings. A software development framework provides a common set of standards for developing software in a specific domain (e.g., healthcare, accounting, communication). It's meant for developers who aren't necessarily interested in developing their custom framework from scratch. Every time they begin work on a new project with different requirements than their last one.

A methodology is an umbrella term for various methods and techniques used in software development. These include everything from Agile methodologies like Scrum, Kanban, and Lean to general waterfall scheduling or pseudo-code documentation techniques. The critical thing to understand about these two concepts differs from what they are. But how they can help you achieve your goals as an individual developer or team leader working within the scope of a larger project or organisation."

What is a Software Development Framework?

A software development framework is a set of guidelines that allows you to build a working version of your product in a shorter time. A framework makes use of existing components and libraries. It includes standard conventions and design patterns for implementing functionality. The general idea behind a framework is that you build on top of proven, existing components.

Software Development Frameworks allow you to focus on your product's unique aspects and save time to re-implement what has already been built repeatedly. In addition, frameworks are generally targeted at large organisations with specific requirements.

What is a Software Development Methodology?

A software development methodology is a generic set of practices and principles that guide software development. There is no one "right way" to develop software, but there are practices that can help make your efforts more efficient and effective. A methodology describes the process you use to build software, including all the steps, activities, and tools involved. There are many different methodologies, each with its strengths and weaknesses. Using a process ensures that your team follows best practices and achieves a consistent result. It can also be helpful to use different methodologies depending on the phase of the project.

Why are Frameworks and Methodologies Important?

Any given project has its unique requirements and constraints. The problem with this is that it means you need a clearer idea of what to do. It would be best if you found a way to narrow down all the possible approaches to select the best one. A software development framework or methodology is one way to do this. A framework or methodology provides a common way to address a specific problem. It includes commonly accepted best practices that have proven effective in many situations. To be more precise, frameworks and methodologies provide the basis for building our solution. Frameworks and methodologies are helpful in several ways:

1. They may give you ready-made components that can save you time.
2. They can help you structure your code consistently, making it easier to maintain.
3. They can help ensure that your solution is compatible with a broader ecosystem.

Benefits of Frameworks and Methodologies

Speed: Software development methodologies and frameworks are well-established processes that help you get your product to market faster. You can focus on the specific needs of your project because you have a set of standard practices to fall back on. In addition, you can reuse other people's code (provided copyrights are allowed and open source) and adapt it to your specific needs. The speed to the market can save you time and money for any organisation.

Consistency: Having a standard way to approach tasks ensures that everyone on your team follows the same conventions and uses the same tools. In addition, consistency in approaches and following standards makes it easier to onboard new team members, transfer knowledge between team members, and increase overall productivity.

Ecosystem alignment: You want your solution to be compatible with other solutions and for end users to accept it. A software development methodology or framework ensures that your software is consistent with the broader ecosystem. For example, the popular programming language PHP has many frameworks that solve everyday problems. They all follow the same basic rules and provide standard solutions. e.g., /- data storage and authentication issues. The result is a more compatible ecosystem where everyone uses the same tools and techniques.

Limitations of Frameworks and Methodologies

No software development approach is perfect. There are trade-offs with every decision and methodology. While frameworks and methodologies can help you achieve consistency and speed, they have the potential to stifle creativity and innovation. It's important to understand that every project has no one-size-fits-all solution. Tailoring your approach to the specific needs of your project and team is key to success. Limitations of software development methodologies and frameworks include

Diversity problem: A significant challenge of software development methodologies is designed to be generic enough to solve various issues. While this is good in many respects, it also means that this methodology cannot account for all situations.

No silver bullet: Every methodology has its strengths and weaknesses. You need to understand that all methodologies have flaws and decide whether they're worth the trade-off for your project.

Differences Between a Framework and Methodology

Focus: A framework focuses on low-level implementation details, such as reusable code components, libraries, data models, and functionality. A methodology is more concerned with the high-level process of developing software. Such as how tasks are prioritised and tracked, what tools are used, and when certain activities occur.

Level of detail: A framework is more general and high-level. It gives you a broad overview of the best approach and available implementation details. On the other hand, a methodology is more specific and low-level. It provides a detailed breakdown of all the tasks you need to accomplish, including how they should be prioritised and tracked.

Benefits of Framework/Methodology Over Custom Code

The advantage of using a software development framework or methodology is that you can start from scratch every time you begin a new project. Instead, you can use existing code tested and used successfully by others. Using a framework or methodology also allows you to focus on the specific needs of your project. Framework or methodology helps you avoid getting bogged down in the implementation details and will enable you to focus on the bigger picture of your project. You can complete your programs more efficiently and with fewer bugs.

When Should You Use a Framework?

A framework is best used for projects where you know what to do and the general path you need to follow to get there. For example, you see the problem you're trying to solve and have decided on a solution. You also have a general idea of how you will implement that solution. In this case, you should use a framework to help you get started and avoid getting lost in the details. A framework gives you a proven approach to tackling a problem. It includes standard libraries and design patterns that you can use to solve specific issues. A framework is less concerned with the specifics of your project and more focused on general best practices.

When Should You Use a Methodology?

A methodology is best used when you need a clear idea of what to do or want to explore the options available. For example, your project is likely in the early stages, and you need to know what you need to do or how you will do it. Or, you know what you want to do but need a clear path to get there. In this case, you should use a methodology to help you dive into the details of your project and select the best approach. A methodology focuses on the high-level process and gives you a general outline of what you need to do. It provides a wide range of options and leaves.

CHAPTER 7: APPLYING THE RIGHT FRAMEWORK AND METHODOLOGY FOR YOUR BEST FIT

- **Framework:** A foundational structure underlying a system, concept, or idea.
- **Methodology:** A discipline's set of methods, rules, and postulates.

Well, from the previous Chapter, you know the differences between Frameworks and methodologies. Is it enough? Not. As We read in the Don't fail to understand the core values chapter, organisations' views about DevOps are filled with many myths and assumptions. What are those myths? I help you to name a few here.

1. DevOps is not fit for SDLC or Waterfall method.
2. DevOps is not for the Legacy environment.
3. DevOps is a one-time effort.
4. DevOps is Agile
5. DevOps Will not be compatible with ITIL
6. DevOps is only for Infrastructure and Development

These perceptions are assumptions and hurdles to slow down the journey. Please remember that DevOps can work with the Waterfall method too! The only thing is that you need to yield the real benefits of DevOps. And in this Chapter, let us crack the code on How are these myths striking us during the initial DevOps Transformation?

After deep diving into the previous chapters, we are familiar with various software development methodologies. In contrast, many around us let us only dive deep into some methods. So let us brief a few latest methodologies here.

Scrum - Scrum is a software development framework that has become popular recently because it is an iterative and incremental process. It is also designed to help teams manage their work. Scrum enables individuals and teams to deliver value incrementally and collaboratively. If you're starting, think of it as a way for your team to make efforts in small chunks, with experimentation and feedback loops.

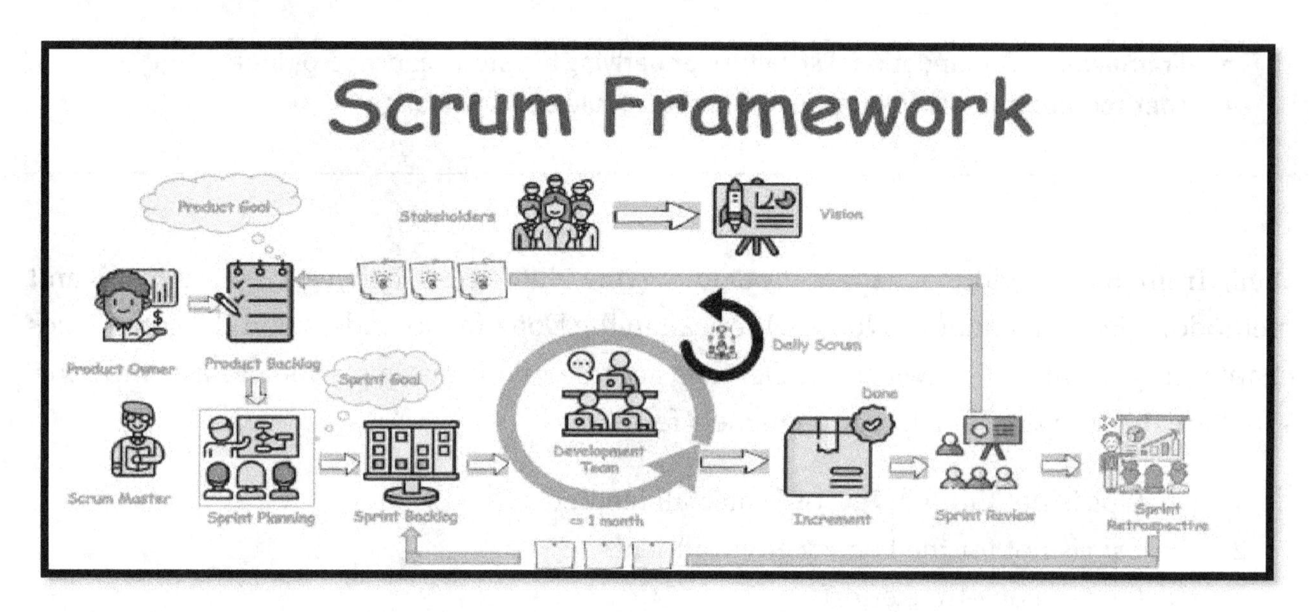

Source: agilemania.com

Scrum's primary goal is to meet the customer's needs by fostering a culture of open communication, shared accountability, and constant improvement. The development process begins with a general understanding of what must be created, developing a list of features prioritised in the product backlog that the product owner wishes to achieve.

The Scrum consists of a Product Owner, a Scrum Master, and Developers, each with specific accountabilities. Trust is a critical Scrum Team characteristic that connects all the elements. Trust in a Scrum Team is necessary for tension and bottlenecks in getting work done.

Agile is a software development framework that promotes a more collaborative approach to software development over other frameworks that might not be as interactive. In addition, it has many inherent practices that encourage continuous software integration, Delivery, and deployment. Unlike other principles,

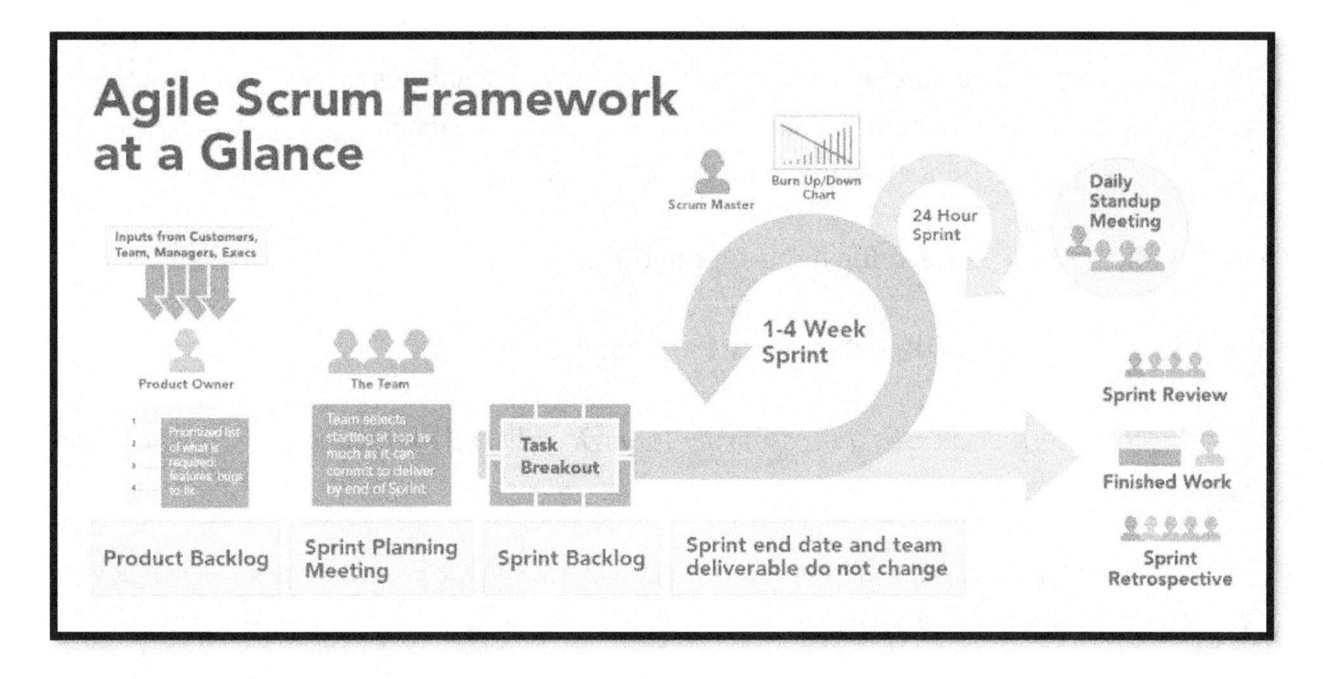

Source: Planview

Agile has a clear manifesto and twelve principles. This helps any organisations wishing to transform into agile will guide them.

The Agile Manifesto outlines the key values and principles governing the Agile philosophy, intending to assist development teams in working more efficiently and sustainably.

Agile Manifesto:

We are uncovering better ways of developing Software by doing it and helping others do it. Through this work, we have come to value:

Individuals and interactions over processes and tools
Working software over comprehensive documentation
Customer collaboration over contract negotiation
Responding to change over following a plan

That is, while there is value in the items on the right, we value the items on the left more.

The Twelve Principles behind the Manifesto

Our highest priority is to satisfy the customer through early and continuous delivery of valuable software.

Welcome changing requirements, even late in development. Agile processes harness change for the customer's competitive advantage.

Deliver working software frequently, from a couple of weeks to a couple of months, with a preference to the shorter timescale.

Business people and developers must work together daily throughout the project.

Build projects around motivated individuals. Give them the environment and support they need, and trust them to get the job done.

The most efficient and effective method of conveying information to and within a development team is face-to-face conversation.

Working software is the primary measure of progress.

Agile processes promote sustainable development. The sponsors, developers, and users should be able to maintain a constant pace indefinitely.

Continuous attention to technical excellence and good design enhances agility.

Simplicity--the art of maximizing the amount of work not done is essential.

The best architectures, requirements, and designs emerge from self-organizing teams.

At regular intervals, the team reflects on how to become more effective, then tunes and adjusts its behavior accordingly.

Source: https://agilemanifesto.org/

Kanban is a system that was initially designed for Lean Manufacturing but can be used in any production process that requires managing the work-in-progress inventory. Some companies are operating their production and operation support using this method. Kanban is a great tool to visualise WIP. So, WIP reduction is greatly possible with the Kanban framework.

A Kanban system offers an organised approach to identifying opportunities for improving efficiency by visually tracking and managing work.

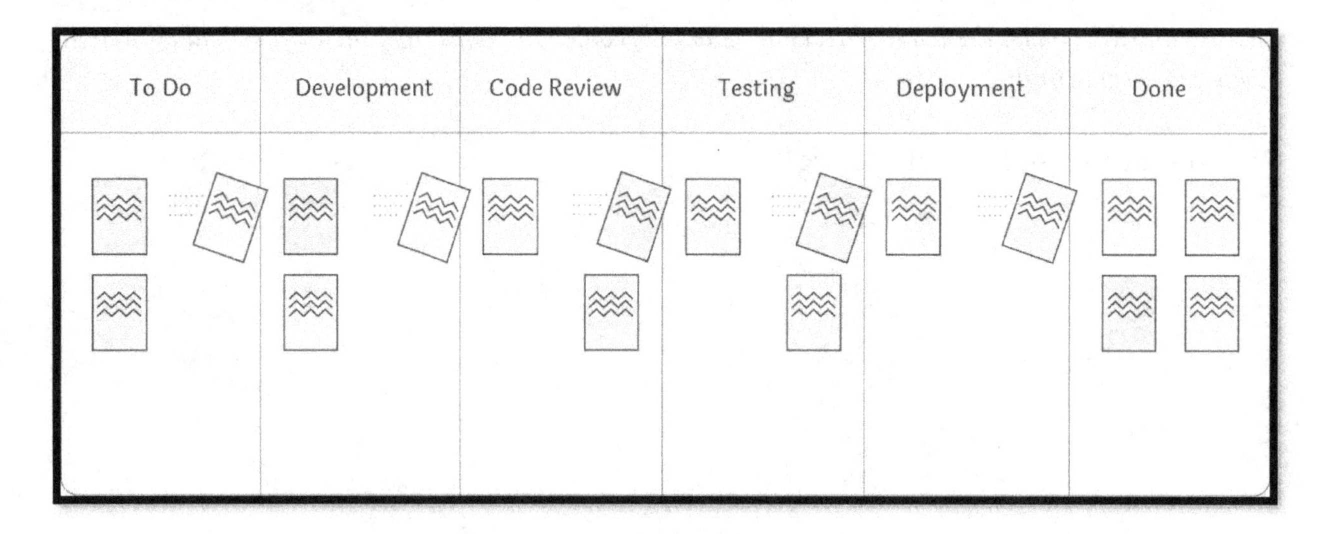

Source: getnave

Scaled Agile Framework (SAFe): The Scaled Agile Framework® (SAFe®) is a collection of organisational and workflow patterns for deploying agile practices at the enterprise level. The framework is a body of knowledge that includes structured guidance on roles and responsibilities, work planning and management, and values to adhere to.

SAFe encourages alignment, collaboration, and delivery across many agile teams. It was built on three fundamental bodies of knowledge: agile software development, lean product development, and systems thinking.

SAFe has one advantage. SAFe offers a systematic approach for scaling agile as businesses grow. It is divided into four configurations to accommodate different levels of scale: Essential SAFe, Large Solution SAFe, Portfolio SAFe, and Full SAFe.

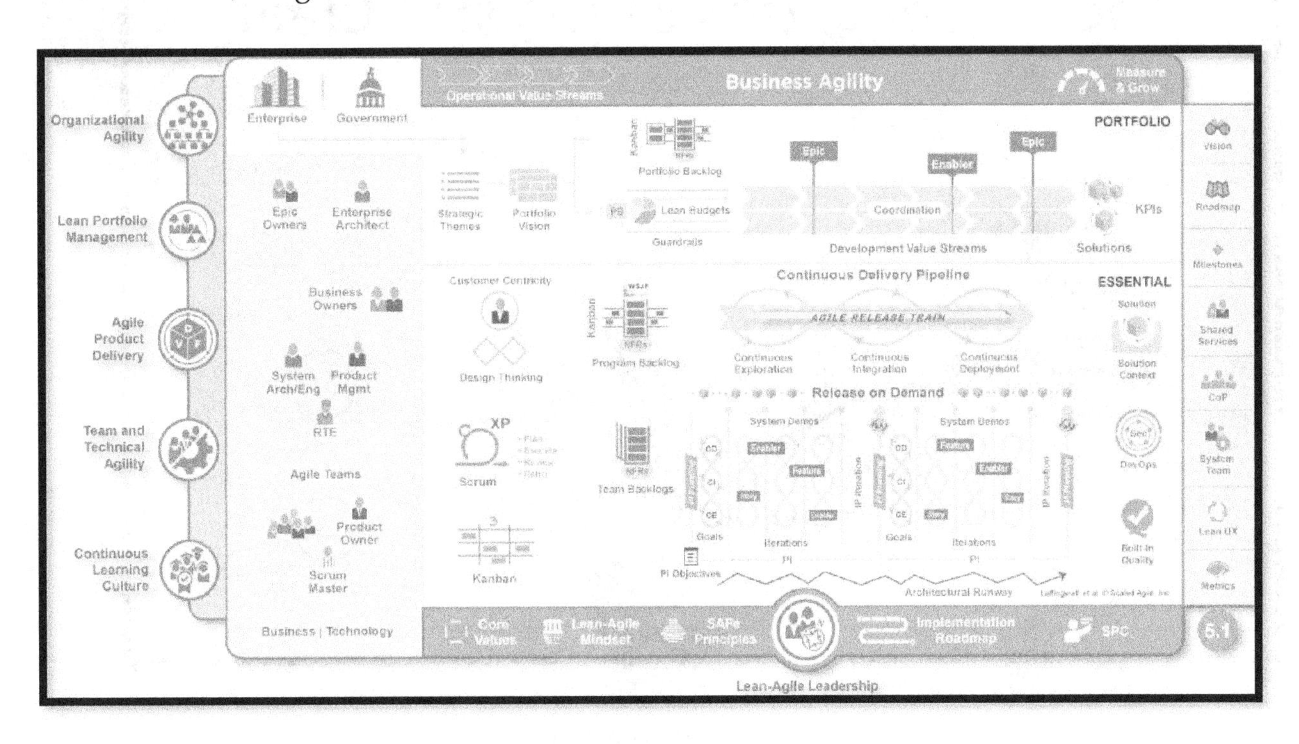

Source: https://www.scaledagileframework.com/

Crystal Clear: is a software solution that centres around creating transparency within a team by outlining the goals and objectives of each team member. Crystal Clear method is designed to help users stay productive, produce quality work, and strive for continuous improvement.

People are the most crucial aspect of Crystal Methods, so processes should be designed to meet the team's needs. It is adaptable because it lacks a set of predefined tools and techniques. It is also light in terms of documentation, management, and reporting. Finally, the project environment and team size determine the methodology's weight. Crystal Clear, for example, is designed for short-term projects by a team of six developers working from a single workspace.

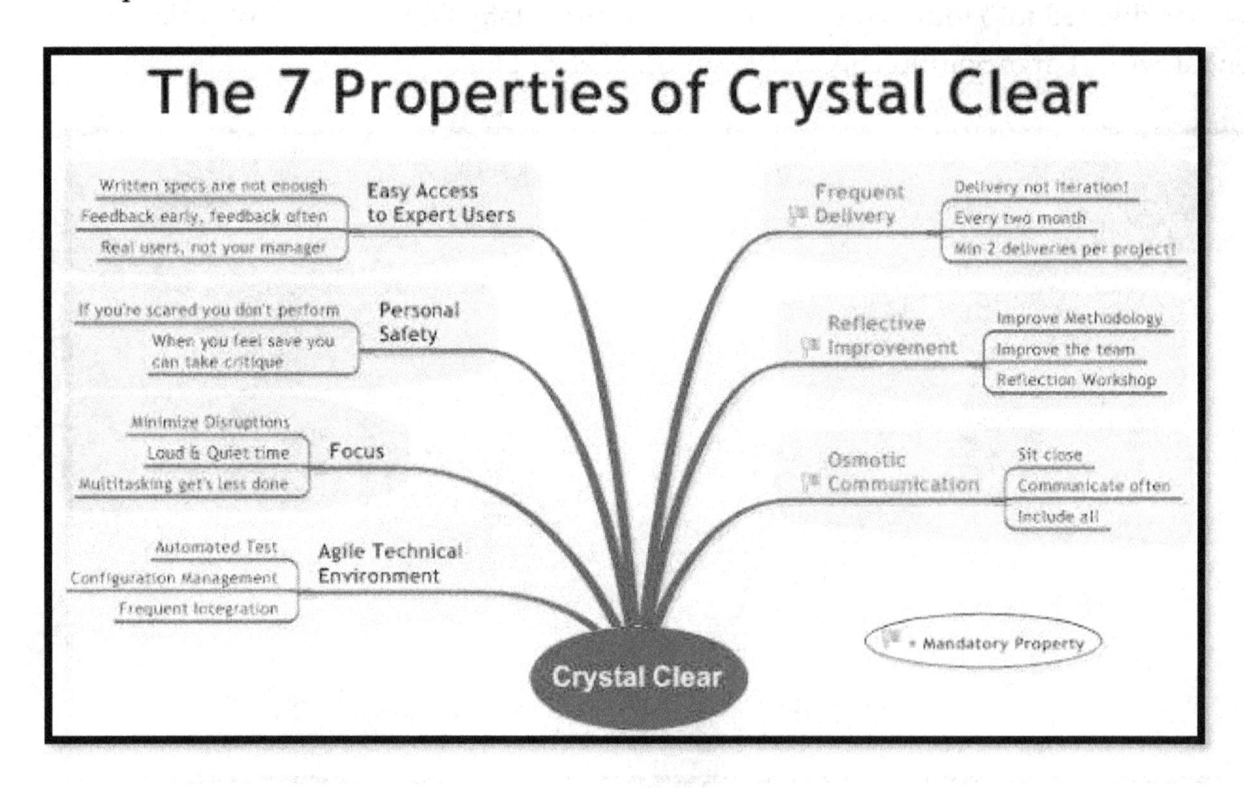

Source: Project-management.com

And a few others, namely, Test-driven development, Design Driven Development, Behavioural driven development and so on. Stay consistent with the chapter objective and focus on how DevOps can work with contemporary Standards such as ITIL/ITSM and Agile, which are widely accepted in every domain.

Let's take Agile First! How can agile work with DevOps Transformation and add value?

Agile and DevOps have been different worlds since they started their lives. Both see software development as a process where the most minor changes are frequently made to improve the code's quality. In addition to that, all these small changes need to be coordinated and tested before being released to customers. But, like any other relationship, these two weren't always rosy. The main difference is that Agile values collaboration and transparency, whereas DevOps values continuous integration and testing as its pillars of existence. Therefore, if you want your DevOps and Agile software development projects to succeed, you will need to change your ways for them to work harmoniously together. Let us have some principles to help you with that.

Plan, don't plan, and then plan again.

Despite the DevOps movement being around for some time, many organisations still use their traditional planning and tracking methodologies while building their new software projects. While this might seem like a good idea, it's a big turn-off for the Agile approach to development. Planning is not only a lost art but also makes no sense in an Agile environment, as you'll find out when you try to build something new and never plan for it. Therefore, if you try to use planning, you'll quickly realise that it doesn't work well with an Agile development project. Plan the features, but different from the way they'll be implemented.

Embrace change

A core premise of DevOps is that you must be open to change and be prepared to change how you do things if needed. Embracing change is especially important if you're part of an Agile project. It might sound a bit strange, but without change and the ability to adapt to new situations, you'll never be able to succeed in an environment where the rules are constantly changing. If you plan your development projects using traditional methods and are afraid to try something new because it will fail, you might as well give up on your software development projects now. You need to embrace change and be open to change if you want to succeed in a DevOps environment. This might mean trying new methods and techniques, but it also means being open to change if your team needs to be more aligned than you had hoped.

Teamwork is more important than tools.

One of the main differences between DevOps and Agile is that DevOps focuses on the people behind the tools and techniques instead of the tools themselves. While tools are essential, they need help to do the job. Instead, they need to be used by people who understand their purpose and how they can leverage it to achieve a common goal.

Agile software development approaches focus on people and their interactions with a project or product. It's about how people work together and collaborate to create software. Therefore, it's about something other than the tools they use. However, it would be best if you still chose the right tools for your development projects. You must select the right software to support your business goals and make your job as a software developer easier. Just remember, it's not about the tool, but it's about the people who are using the tool.

Communicate clearly with your team and stakeholders

Agile development projects focus on communication between the team members and stakeholders. Communication can include customers, managers, and product owners, among others. DevOps, on the other hand, is about bridging the gap between the development and operations teams by implementing tools that make communication and collaboration easier. Both teams need to have a clear understanding of the goals and intentions of each other. This means communicating frequently and clearly with each other. If you want your software development projects to succeed, you must have a clear vision and message for your stakeholders. In addition to that, you need to understand their needs and expectations. If you can do that, you can ensure that the product you release to your customers is what they want and need.

Test, test, test some more.

Once you understand the requirements of your stakeholders, it's time to start coding and testing your product; this seems common sense. But many organisations need to test their software before releasing it to customers. Sound like a waste of time and money? But testing your software before release can save your team much time, which will significantly help reduce the cost of poor quality and technical debt fixing costs. Please remember that fixing a bug is costlier than producing a feature for your customer. It's also the cheapest way to find minor issues and bugs before they go out to your customers. You don't need to spend days or weeks testing your software if you start early and stretch frequently. As an Agile development team, you need to focus on releasing code continually and often testing your code before releasing it to customers.

Embrace failure as a learning experience

When building software, we always want to see the project through to the end. We want to see the final product and know that everything we did was worth it. However, many of us are afraid of failing, and we don't want to accept that we might have done something wrong. Therefore, we may give up before we even start. Is it a bit pessimistic? Of course, this is a big problem in the software development world. Many organisations fail when they fail simply because they don't want to accept that they might have made a mistake. This is called cognitive bias, which can be dangerous in software development.

In a nutshell, DevOps is a movement that focuses on the people and the tools used to deliver software projects. On the other hand, Agile development is a more relaxed and collaborative approach to building software that focuses on understanding stakeholders' requirements and building software according to those requirements. Both approaches have their benefits and disadvantages and will succeed in different software development contexts.

Now let us look at How DevOps can perform in ITIL/ITSM Environments.

DevOps with ITIL

DevOps is the marriage of software development and IT operations. The goal is to build and release code with minimal delays, test that code in a virtual environment before it is deployed to production, and keep IT operations working efficiently by automating processes. In other words, DevOps is about collaboration between developers and IT ops professionals. Reading about everything you need to know about DevOps with ITIL will help you further your adoption plans.

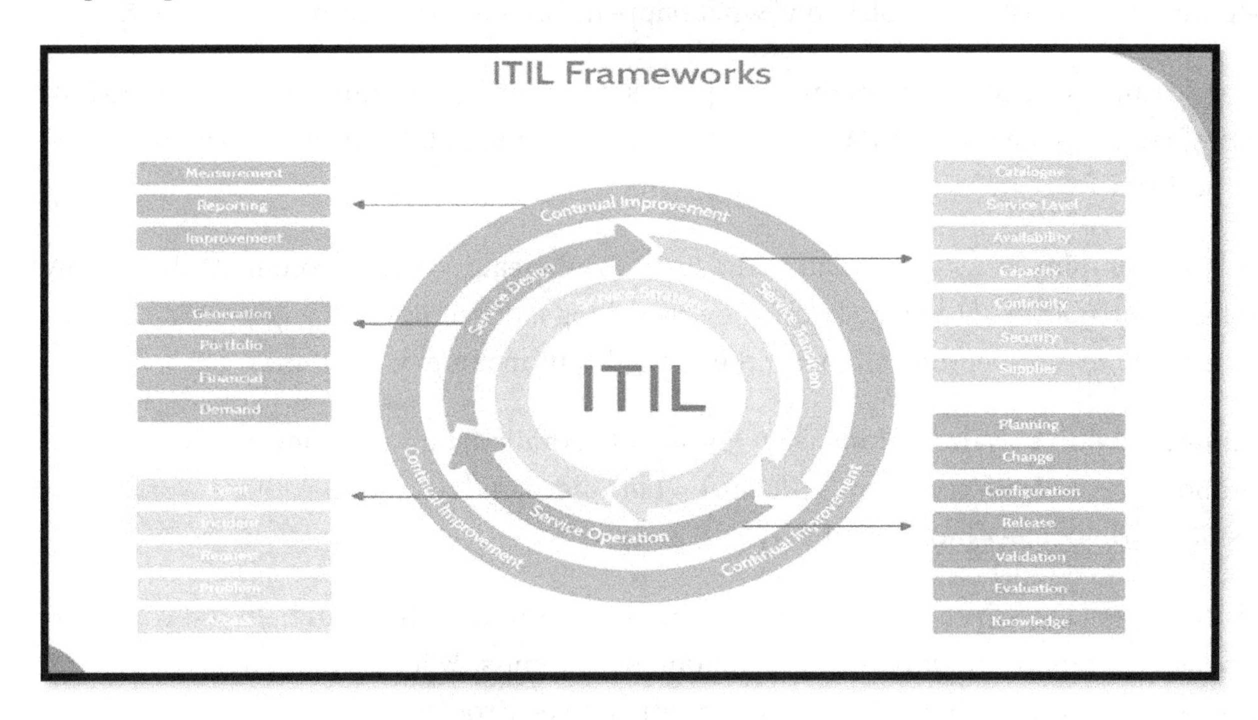

Source: process street

Advantages of adopting DevOps with ITIL

Increased efficiency: DevOps allows you to streamline your operations processes by automating many manual tasks. In other words, DevOps helps increase efficiency by eliminating delays.

Better customer engagement: DevOps combines operations and development and automates many tasks. With a continuous process in place, operations can focus on responding to customers' needs instead of solely on "what happens" in the production environment.

Better hiring practices: Automating the processes reduces new hires' needs. Because the existing team can handle more work while improving their skill set with each automation they perform.

Increased employee engagement: DevOps helps create an environment that allows employee satisfaction. Hirelings know they're making a difference and enjoy their jobs more because they're not spending all their time "doing" but "making" something.

Extended customer satisfaction: DevOps is collaborating between development and IT operations teams. With continuous processes, both sides understand the other's work and, as a result, work together more effectively.

Reduced costs: DevOps is about creating virtual environments that can help test code upon every single commit by developers or automatic commits. With virtual environments, it's possible to test code without affecting the production environment.

Better code quality: With shorter time frames between code releases, bugs get caught and eliminated faster. As a result, you get higher-quality code.

After a look at the advantages of adopting DevOps in the ITIL environment, it's also worth flipping the page and looking at the other side, so that, while you are implementing DevOps Journey in your organisation, you will take careful steps.

Disadvantages of adopting DevOps with ITIL

Operational Complexities: DevOps creates new operational complexity by breaking the silos between development and operations teams. The teams may need help understanding each other because they need to get used to talking and having their language. These behaviours lead to new operational complexities like managing team interdependencies and conflicting priorities. But, if you are mindful of this measure with proper mitigation, this will turn into an excellent communication platform by removing silos.

Lack of visibility: One of the biggest challenges with DevOps is the need for more visibility between development and operations teams. This means you must learn how your code works or what's happening with your infrastructure. As a result, operations teams could be affected by the code releases or feel overwhelmed by the new tasks DevOps requires.

Requirements for an Effective DevOps with ITIL Collaboration.

After skimming through the Advantages and disadvantages of DevOps in the ITIL environment, we can now table the requirements for effective DevOps Implementation in the ITSM/ITIL environments.

Clear definition of roles: DevOps with ITIL requires that the development and operations teams clearly define the roles and responsibilities of each member. For example, each team member should understand the scope of their responsibilities and have their work clearly defined.

Communication: More than just defining roles and responsibilities, communication is key to effective collaboration between development and operations. Indicates that both teams must talk to each other and explain their work.

Trust: Trust is crucial to collaboration between development and operations teams. Trust is built as each team member explains their work, the work of other team members, and the project manager's work.

Shared Vision: Are both teams working toward the same goal? If so, then a shared vision can help define and achieve that goal.

You are now halfway thru of your ITIL Literacy. Upon skimming the basic principles of ITIL, as a reader, now your curiosity will grow about how to achieve core concepts of ITIL and DevOps. So why do we need to leave that question unattended? Let's see how we can perform this.

How to Achieve Continuous Integration (DevOps) With ITIL?

Establish a transparent product management structure: A clear project management structure is crucial to successful DevOps with ITIL. This structure should include product envisioning, project managers, documentation, and a clear product timeline and roadmap.

Create a project data management framework: DevOps with ITIL relies on project data management to help manage project data, which includes project files, project information, project artefacts, and project reports.

Create a project tool management framework: Each project must use a consistent project management tool. This tool should help you manage the project implemented with it.

Define and enforce project standards: DevOps with ITITL requires that all project activities be performed according to defined criteria, including using standards-based tools and processes.

Establish a project governance framework: Project governance should include effective risk management, change management, and compliance management.

Establish a project monitoring framework: Continuous and automatic monitoring tools are essential to DevOps with ITIL.

Establish a project configuration management framework: Configuration management and its principles must be followed for all project artefacts.

Maintain a project quality management framework: Quality management should be used for all project activities to ensure quality outcomes. There should be no compromises of the quality metrics and predetermined quality outcomes.

Continuous Delivery (DevOps)

Continuous integration (CI): this is when all code is tested automatically regularly. Continuous integration is an essential foundation for DevOps with ITIL.

Continuous Delivery (CD): this is where code is released to production regularly. Continuous Delivery is the final stage of the DevOps process, and the release is automated. So Must have, clear metrics and quality gates must be set before formal release.

CD/CD-hybrid: In some cases, you might use a hybrid approach where you release code regularly with automated testing but also use a quality gate process to reject code that isn't good enough

Well, we are almost done. Before concluding this Chapter, look at the benefits of DevOps with ITIL.

The Benefits of DevOps with ITIL

Faster code: Releases happen faster as developers work with a continuous process and test the code in a virtual environment before it's deployed to production.

Fewer code defects: Code releases are more likely to be free of bugs as they're tested in a virtual environment before they're deployed to production.

Reduced defect rates: Code releases are less likely to be buggy as they're tested in a virtual environment before they're deployed to production.

Standardised practices: Code releases are more likely to follow standardised practices. So, for example, if the code standards are followed, then code releases are more likely to follow the standards.

CHAPTER 8: ESTABLISH FEEDBACK LOOPS

Feedback: Information or scrutiny is given to someone or something to improve performance, product, etc.

When DevOps and Agile work together, they form a strong feedback loop that helps your team continuously improve processes and products. These two methods, working in parallel and together to bring new software to market faster and with less risk, are collaborative approaches to software development. However, only some organisations utilise DevOps or Agile. By connecting these two processes, you create a feedback loop.

Many only adopt one of these methodologies while neglecting the other. When this happens, there is no continuous improvement cycle between DevOps and Agile or vice versa; each is a standalone practice with limited effectiveness. This Chapter will explain why and how to implement both principles in your organisation. Hence, they create an effective feedback loop for your DevOps Transformation Journey.

What is a DevOps Feedback Loop?

A DevOps feedback loop is a continuous cycle of improvement between the DevOps and Agile practices that helps teams deliver software of better quality, with higher performance, and at a lower cost. The feedback loop must consist of three steps: Analyse, Improve, and Repeat. These steps apply to both DevOps and Agile practices. During the analysis step, teams look at data that includes the metrics of their software delivery processes, including metrics around time to market, release cycles, and customer satisfaction.

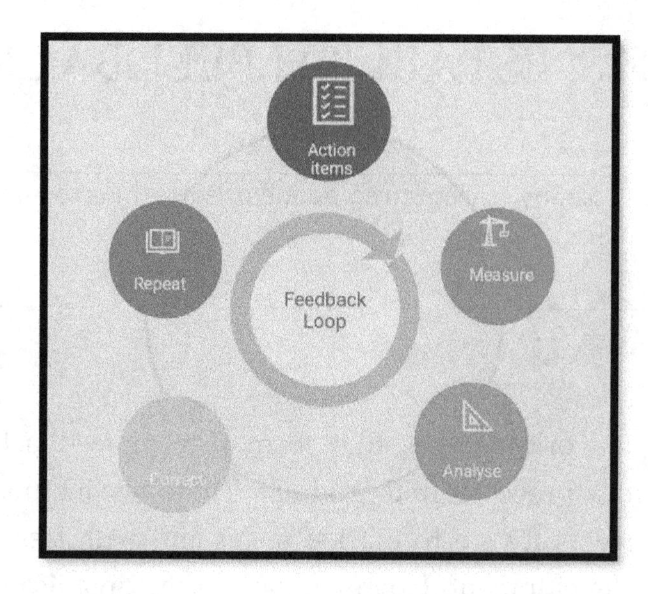

The collected data then use to identify opportunities to improve. During the improvement step, the team must choose one or more areas to focus on for improvement. This could include improving the efficiency of one of the Agile roles or the effectiveness of one of the DevOps practices. Based on the outcome, The team then creates an action plan for how to carry out the improvement, executes that plan, and then monitors the improvement results. Finally, during the repeat step, teams evaluate the effectiveness of the progress and decide whether to keep the adjustment or make other changes for continuous improvement. Some of the Key items are not limited to the listed below to include in the action plan.

a. Action Items
b. Owner of the action item
c. ETA to Complete the action item
d. Next review

What is an Agile Feedback Loop?

This segment is recurrent of the last part! By this time, readers would realise the similarities and differences between agile but worth reading.

An agile feedback loop is a continuous improvement cycle between Agile practices such as metrics, collaboration, and culture. That helps teams deliver software of higher quality at a faster rate while also decreasing risk. These steps apply to both DevOps and Agile practices. For example, during the analysis step, teams look at data that includes their software delivery processes, metrics around time to market, release cycles, and customer satisfaction.

This data will be more beneficial in identifying opportunities to improve. During the improvement step, the team chooses one or more areas to focus on for improvement. These activities include improving the efficiencies of the Agile roles such as testing. Or the effectiveness of one of the DevOps practices (such as automation).

The team then creates an action plan for how to carry out the improvement, executes that plan, and then monitors the improvement results. Finally, during the repeat step, teams evaluate the effectiveness of the advance and decide whether to keep the adjustment or make other changes for continuous improvement.

How to Build a DevOps Feedback Loop?

When building a DevOps feedback loop, there are a few key areas to focus on, including:

Adopt the right culture and mindset: Leaders must embrace the new way of working. They must communicate openly and honestly with employees, trust them to do their jobs, and provide them with the tools and resources they need to succeed.

Adopt the right tools and processes for the job: Tools like automation, monitoring, and configuration management help teams move more quickly and effectively. But, of course, culture and mindset are equally important.

However, a DevOps feedback loop will only be effective with adopting the right tools and processes for the job.

- Support the right people on the team
- Business leaders must support hiring the right people and giving them the resources, they need to succeed.

This means supporting hiring the right talent, providing employees with the training they need, and offering them the mentorship they require to be successful.

DevOps and the Importance of Feedback Loops

Feedback loops are essential to the DevOps Journey, helping teams understand how well they are performing and where they can improve. Unfortunately, organisations that only implement one of these methodologies often miss out on both benefits. With a feedback loop between DevOps and Agile, teams may understand how well they perform and what areas they can improve.

They may need to see that they are clashing or even working together. For example, suppose an organisation only implements DevOps without Agile. In that case, it may miss out on the benefits of collaboration and fail to identify opportunities for continuous improvement. On the other hand, if an organisation only implements Agile with DevOps, it may not know that it needs to meet customer needs and delivery goals.

Why is a DevOps and Agile Feedback Loop important?

Feedback loops are essential for two reasons:

- They help you understand how well you are doing. Feedback loops allow organisations to learn from their mistakes and successes to continuously improve their processes, products, and services.
- They support a collaborative culture. For instance, feedback loops allow organisations to work together, not just beside one another. They also help organisations share information, support each other, and identify areas where they can improve.

How does a Feedback Loop Create Continual Improvement in DevOps and Agile?

There are two main ways a feedback loop creates continual improvement in DevOps and Agile:

Feedback loops help you identify areas for continuous improvement. Continuous improvement is about being aware of the current state and identifying areas for improvement. A feedback loop makes it easier to understand where your organisation excels and where it might struggle.

Feedback loops foster collaboration between DevOps and Agile practices. When the two practices work together, they create a feedback loop that feeds back information. This includes metrics on the state of the overall organisation. And information on how successful each practice is in achieving its goals.

Creating a Continuous Improvement Culture Through DevOps and Agile Together

Organisations can create a continuous improvement culture that benefits everyone by making a feedback loop between DevOps and Agile. Continual improvement practices are critical when organisations are growing and changing or undergoing a transformation. A feedback loop between DevOps and Agile creates an open and transparent culture that fosters collaboration and helps everyone understand how they contribute to the organisation. It also allows organisations to identify areas for continuous improvement and create action plans to achieve those goals.

In a Nutshell, it's crucial to implement concepts from both DevOps and Agile when it comes to improving your software delivery processes. A feedback loop between these practices helps teams identify areas for improvement, collaborate more effectively, and create a continuous improvement culture that benefits everyone. Feedback loops are essential for two reasons. First, they allow organisations to learn from their mistakes and successes to improve their processes, products, and services continuously. And they help foster a collaborative culture.

PART 3 – MOKITAS IN THE AUTOMATION ROOM

CHAPTER 1: TOOLS SELECTION TRICK

Tools Selection Strategy: Using a variety of tools and techniques to assess the current state of a business environment and plan for its future.

The most critical of every DevOps Transformation Journey is tool selection. Tools and Technologies are not only driving automation; they need to deal with Change, incidents, problems, release, test case management, source control etc. Unfortunately, sometimes this will be a trap too! In the chapter, let's take a wholesale look at the Best DevOps Tools Selection Strategies and The Impact of Poorly Selected Tools and Considerations Before Selecting the Right Choices of Tools.

In today's fast-paced, competitive business environment, organisations need to find ways to innovate and stay ahead of the game. To develop and deliver faster, they need to adopt a DevOps culture. Choosing the right DevOps tools is the best way to keep your organisation on the cutting edge.

Here are some tips to help you choose the right DevOps tools for your transformation:

1. Invest in software that supports your company's strategy
2. Ensure that your software integrates with other applications
3. Choose features that will make it easy for you to integrate new processes and technologies into your workflow
4. Evaluate how well the software will fit with development teams and individuals who use it
5. Research reviews from other companies that have made similar investments

In the transformation Journey, DevOps is an organisation that facilitates faster software development processes, shorter release cycles, and continuous software quality testing. With this accelerated pace of software production and testing, you must find the right tools for your team. Next, you must pick the best DevOps tools that support your team's processes and workflow. But how do you know which ones are the best? There are many factors to consider when selecting the right DevOps tools for your organisation. The list of available options is almost endless, making it challenging to choose which one will work best for your team or company. You need to understand what these tools can do for you, what they won't be able to do, and everything in between before making a final decision in the tight business deadlines and Competition. Unfortunately, some organisations forget to follow the right strategies and select the wrong shortcut route to choose the right tools.

In this chapter, let us explore what all those blind spots and biases are

Basics first, before deep diving, Let's look at what DevOps Tool is. And why is it important?

What is a DevOps tool?

A DevOps tool is a software application used for automating tasks and processes. They are integral to your continuous integration/delivery (CI/CD) pipeline. In the software development lifecycle to help you deliver high-quality products faster. In addition, these tools help with various aspects of your software operations. It can include managing the configuration of your infrastructure and the software installed on it, sharing resources across your team, tracking defects and errors, and monitoring performance metrics.

Now take a view on What organisations are usually unknowingly trapped by missing the essential objectives of the Tools selection strategy and how to perform those necessary métiers.

Why Are DevOps Tools Important?

These days, organisations need to find ways to innovate and stay ahead of the game to survive. Adopting a DevOps culture is the best way to keep your organisation on the cutting edge. The best way to do that is by choosing the right DevOps tools.

The first step is choosing software that supports your company's strategy. This software should enable you to work smarter and more efficiently as an organisation. You want software that will integrate with other applications, but choose features that will make it easy for you to incorporate new processes and technologies into your workflow. You also want software that will be easy for development teams and individuals who use it daily. And finally, research reviews from other companies who have made similar investments. So, you can see if their experience matches your expectations before purchasing.

Defining your Organisation's requirements

Before researching and evaluating the various DevOps tools available, you must define your organisation's requirements. What problems need to be solved? What are the goals of this tool selection? To do this, you must go back to the beginning and look at your organisation's needs. What is the purpose of your DevOps initiative?

What specific needs does your organisation need to address with these tools? What is the current state of your software development lifecycle? By addressing these questions and more, you can understand the requirements of the tools you will need to select for your organisation.

Take Time to Understand the Benefits of Each Tool.

Once you've defined your requirements, it's time to start looking at the available DevOps tools and understanding what they can do for you. Each tool will have its benefits, but there might be better fits for your organisation. To make an informed decision, you need to go through each tool and understand what it can do for you and your team. For example, you may need some way to manage access to shared resources across your team. You may have multiple people working on the same database and need a way to track who has what access.

The Price Is Only the Deciding Factor.

Organisations are usually tempted to select the cheapest tools, but that is only sometimes the best decision. While price should be factored in when deciding, you must also consider the tool's long-term impact and cost. Will it be able to meet your needs for the long term? Will the tool be cost-effective when managing it over a long time? Other factors, such as ease of use, may make a more expensive tool more worthwhile in the long run.

How Will You Measure Success?

Please also consider the success rates associated with each tool you're considering. For example,

1. How effective is this tool in solving your organisation's problems?
2. How many issues have been resolved or managed by this tool?
3. How many problems have managed to slip through the cracks?

The above questions will give you an idea of how successful software has been for other organisations. You can then determine if that success rate will be sufficient for your organisation.

What to Look for When Selecting DevOps Tools?

Scalability and reliability: You need to select tools that can grow with your organisation. They must be scalable to support your growing team and provide enough functionality to meet your future needs. They also need to be reliable enough to support your team.

Support for open standards: You want to select tools that are open and able to work with other tools. They need to be able to communicate with other vendors' tools and not be proprietary. They also need to be open so that you can integrate them with your existing tools and systems.

Ease of use: You want an easy tool for your team. It should be simple enough that it does not require excessive training or documentation. It should also be easy to integrate into your organisation's workflow. -

Ability to integrate with other software: You want to select a tool that can integrate with your existing software to automate specific tasks. It should also be able to integrate with other vendors' software.

Due to the dynamic nature of the business, Organisations often tend to skip some of the critical tool selection strategies. So, what are the Most Important Criteria for Selecting Tools?

While there are many criteria to consider when selecting tools, a few are the most important. These include scalability, reliability, and support for open standards. You also want to look at the ease of use and the ability to integrate with other software. Another important criterion is cost. You want to ensure you select the tools within your organisation's budget. You also want to consider the overall cost of ownership. This Activity ensures you can sustain your tools and remain within your budget over the long term.

What are the Most Common Mistakes in DevOps Tool Selection?

Organisations make a few common mistakes when selecting tools for their DevOps initiatives. The first is trying to choose one tool to do everything. Tools are very specialised, and you will likely find one that can do everything you need. It would help if you were realistic and selected tools designed to meet specific needs.

The second mistake is selecting a tool due to its hype or the associated sales pitch. You need to be realistic about the functionality of these tools and choose the one that is the best fit for your organisation and its needs.

Let's choose the right way to select the tools that fit your purpose.

Assessing your current tools

Before you start selecting new tools, you also need to assess your current tools. What is working well? What needs to fix? Why is it, or isn't it working? So first, you need to understand what your current tools are doing for you and what they cannot do. With this, you know your weaknesses and what you need to address. It will allow you to identify the gaps in your processes and workflow. It will also give you a better understanding of how the new tools will fit into your organisation.

Assessing current processes and workflow

You also need to assess your current processes and workflow. Few areas that you may consider

How are you currently handling your software development lifecycle? What tools are you now exist in your Ecosystem?

1. What do those tools do?
2. What can they do?
3. What can they not do?

While you have the blueprint of that list, you can understand what you need from new tools by assessing your current tools. You can identify gaps in your workflow, determine where tools are falling short, and discover areas that need improvement. This holistic mapping exercise will also help you understand what new tools can do for you.

Using your tools to improve your processes

Now that you have identified the gaps in your current tools, it's time to see where you can improve. First, you need to place a process or workflow that needs to be fixed for you and then take steps to improve it.

For example, suppose the process or workflow needs to generate the anticipated results. In that case, I recommend looking at why this is happening. If that's not an issue, look at other areas of your business. Doing this will give you a clear understanding of what needs to be done to develop a better process or workflow. In addition, this will help you identify areas of improvement and help you determine which specific areas need attention.

Using new tools as part of your overall business strategy

If any areas are missing from your current toolset, that may be a step in the right direction. A plan can also be a part of your company's overall strategy. An organisation's technology strategy should include specific objectives and goals to fulfil the organisation's overall business strategy.

For example, as part of the organisation's objectives and goals in utilising new tools. Organisations should avoid wasting time dealing with old or existing processes and moving forward with the products and services.

Let me name a few recommendations to select the right tools for your DevOps Transformation.

The importance of integration

A significant consideration in choosing the right DevOps tools is how well the software will integrate with other applications in your ecosystem. For example, suppose your organisation has many different applications. In that case, you need to find solutions that will work seamlessly with them.

It's also important to choose features that will allow your organisation to integrate new processes and technologies into your workflow. As technological advancement changes, the requirements for businesses change accordingly. You want to ensure that your software can adapt and adjust as these changes happen so your company can stay up with the Competition. The last thing you want is for your software to get outdated because it can't handle new requirements.

Finally, ensure that any DevOps tools you choose are compatible with development teams and individuals who use them regularly. As mentioned earlier, developments in technology require adjustments in business strategy. Also, the employees who work in operation must consult when choosing software, as they will be responsible for making changes when necessary.

Choosing the right features

Your software needs to be able to integrate with other applications and processes. For example, suppose you want to use your software for simple process automation. In that case, your software does not need the same features as a company that wants to utilise it for DevOps.

It's also vital that the software you choose has all the necessary features for your company. For instance, can it support development teams and individuals who use it entirely? If not, then that could cause more friction in your workflow.

The reviews from other companies will help you determine how well the software fits with others who have made similar investments. Therefore, it is strongly recommended that you check the reviews to see if there are any complaints or frustrations expressed by other companies who have used this software. You can avoid making a costly mistake.

Evaluate your investment in DevOps tools

There are many options when it comes to DevOps tools. You've probably already realised that you need to consider your company's strategy before deciding on the best software for your needs. It would help if you also thought about how easy the software would be to integrate into your workflow. It should be easy for people within your organisation and those who use it to adapt. You also want to research reviews from companies that have made similar investments to know what other organisations have experienced with the same software.

CHAPTER 2: PROCESS WASTAGES AND UNWANTED WORKFLOWS

Process Wastage: Any action in your process that fails to add value to your customer

Don't fail to Remember the Mokitas!

First, what are Mokitas? And how is this chapter Linked to? Mokitas means "The elephant in the room!" I want to apply this concept to removing process wastage. At the same time, removing or getting the unwanted process out from your ecosystem. It would be best if you needed courage enough.

MOKITAS = PROCESS WASTAGES. But in the DevOps Transformation process, remember these Mokitas will be invisible in your process workflows.

When it comes to a software delivery lifecycle, things can always be streamlined; automated are made more efficient. But unfortunately, most companies only get past the first few stages of development and see small changes here and there. As a result, they only make significant changes impacting the entire lifecycle and how they develop and deploy software. As a result, redesigning ideas for process waste reduction in software automation and delivery can take some work. After all, we're talking about a lot of different elements here. But the good news is that almost every company will have some process. And if you do not, then this is your opportunity to implement one from scratch before moving forward with any other DevOps transformation activities.

Define your core values

Before you do anything else to begin your process waste reduction activities, you need to sit down and develop a core set of values. This will govern the entire process and be the foundation for everything else in your transformation process. These values should be both meaningful to your team and relevant to the work you are doing.

For example, suppose your product is designed to help people. A core value could be "Our product makes people's lives easier." Or suppose you're working for a healthcare company. A core value could be "Our product makes medical professionals' lives easier."

Define your processes

Now that you have your core values, it's time to turn them into processes. What do these values mean when it comes to what your team is doing daily? Are any steps in the software delivery lifecycle redundant or not adding value? Are there any steps that can automate? These are things that should be the basis of the processes you create. For example, suppose one of your Organisation's core values is that product makes people's lives easier. In that case, one of your processes might be that you only create new features when they make people's lives easier. One of your processes could be that you version your code to go back and fix reported bugs quickly.

Define an immutable software architecture

One thing that needs to be talked about more when it comes to software development is architecture. But it's a crucial element for any team, and it can vastly improve it with the right amount of attention. Organisations might consider creating a design architecture for the product from the ground up. Creating an architecture design can achieve as a team exercise where an organisation can define the various parts of their product and what they accomplish. This holistic view and its associated activities will help your Organisation to standardise its processes when it comes to design choices. It will allow any Organisation to have a single source of truth for what their product is made up of. Defining an immutable software architecture is crucial in designing and helping the Organisation with the next item on our list.

Standardise your tools and platforms

One thing that can become incredibly messy in any organisation is its tooling and platform choices. Data, design, testing, and code platforms will vary depending on the team member and the project they are working on. This is all fine if you are working on a single project, but what happens when you have multiple projects? If two projects are using two different data platforms, how will you be able to integrate them? Or what if you have a team member stuck on an older code version, and the rest of the team is using a newer one? You can see how this can quickly snowball into having to do many workarounds that shouldn't need to be there. These are all things that can avoid by implementing standardisation across the board.

Automate as much as possible

This is one of the most significant process wastes that teams need to eliminate. Automating as much as possible is crucial for shortening software delivery lifecycles and bringing consistency to your team members. What can your team automate? Does your data platform automatically update after adding a new data source to your lifecycle? Does your testing software automatically know what to test and how to test it? These are things that you should be looking at as you start to gain a better understanding of your current process. You want to automate as much as possible because it will help reduce human error and provide consistency across the board. This is especially important if your DevOps Transformation is in a larger institution where each team uses different methods to do the same thing.

Build A Continuous Delivery Pipeline

We've discussed a few elements of process waste that can eliminate. Now, it's time to start bringing them all together into a single continuous delivery pipeline. Getting the Core Teams into a single Continuous Delivery pipeline is crucial in software delivery and automation. You should already have it in your sights. As you know, DevOps is a Single piece of flow. But if organisations don't, now is the time to start with some basic Questions.

1. What does the continuous delivery pipeline look like?
2. Is it an automated process triggered whenever code is committed to a designated repository?
3. Are there tests that need to run before that code commit?
4. Are there approvals that need to pass before the code is scheduled to deploy to production?

These questions will help you better to understand the current state of your continuous delivery pipeline and start working towards a better future.

Implement Automated Testing

You may have noticed that automated testing is listed after automating as much as possible. The reason for that is simple. Start automating as many tasks as possible to reduce the time spent on manual tasks. When implementing automated testing, organisations' focus should be ensuring that they only focus on covering what needs to test. There is no sense in trying something that has already been tested manually. Automated testing is about more than just unit tests. Organisations also want to ensure that their software can handle edge cases and that their application functions appropriately when different things happen. They can create automated acceptance tests or integrate their testing software with bug or issue-tracking software.

Implement Intelligent Defect Detection

It's one that almost every team in an institution will benefit from the previous item of our inventory. But it's something that is only sometimes at the top of people's minds when trying to reduce process waste in their organisations. What does intelligent defect detection mean? You are leveraging tools and technologies to detect defects in your code that standard testing might miss; This includes testing against different environments and configurations or monitoring for code issues in real-time. What does this have to do with process waste reduction? Well, it means that you can save time manually testing for these issues.

Establish Better Software Rotations

This one is a little different from the rest. But it's vital and worth considering establishing better software rotations. What does that mean? Well, it's all about ensuring every team member in an institution gets a chance to work on various projects. It's essential to do this because it will help to ensure that the team members are not getting too specialised and can keep their skills up to date. It will also help to ensure that the team members are not burnt out by continuously working on one project.

Reduce reliance on manual labour

this last item is about reducing your team members' manual labour. We're not saying you should remove all human interaction from the equation. However, it would help if you looked for ways to eliminate as much manual labour as possible. What types of manual work do team members perform? Are there ways to automate those tasks or use tools to make them more efficient? This is something that you should keep in mind when you are making your design architecture choices and designing your processes. Redesigning ideas for process waste reduction in software automation and delivery can take some work. After all, we're talking about a lot of different elements here. But the good news is that almost every company will have some sort.

CHAPTER 3: STRUCTURING AUTOMATION

Automation: Technique, Process, Method, or System for entirely intuitive operation or control of a process.

Today's DevOps transformation landscape is more dynamic than ever, and the pace of change continues to accelerate. To stay competitive, businesses must continuously innovate and find ways to streamline processes and standardise operations.

What's the best way to achieve this? Automation. Every company's various processes are on the verge of being streamlined through automation. However, implementing an automation strategy requires a structure to avoid chaos and failure. Unfortunately, here is where most organisations are failing. So, Let's look at why you need to build structure into your automation strategies and explain how you can do so easily.

Organizational Change is the Key to Successful Automation

It's impossible to underestimate the extent of change that automation requires on an organisational and cultural level. Suppose you need to make the change process a priority. You'll likely never see the kind of return on investment from automation that you need. On the other hand, you want your automation strategy to succeed. In that case, you must first invest in the organisational change required for it to happen. When designing your automation strategies, you must consider the human element and analyse the organisational and cultural implications. You need to ensure that you have the right people in the right place to manage and implement the change and that they have the support they need to succeed in

Defining Your Strategy and Objectives

Before you can put your automation strategies in place, it's crucial that you first understand the strategy behind them and the objectives you want to achieve through them. To do so, you must first conduct a thorough business analysis. Start by looking at the current state of your business and the processes in place. Next, outline the goals and objectives you want to achieve through automation. You should also consider the current state of your employees – their skills, experience, and workloads. This Deep dive will give you a clear idea of the type of automation you need to implement and the methods and technologies you can use. Once you know your strategy, you can create the themes and roadmaps for your automation initiatives. Creating a roadmap will help prioritise the most crucial initiatives and help you achieve your objectives within the correct timeframes.

Establishing Themes and Roadmaps

Themes and roadmaps are valuable tools that help you prioritise and align your automation initiatives to achieve your objectives. For each theme, you'll need to outline the goals and objectives you want to achieve and the technologies required. These themes will vary from business to business. For instance, a financial organisation will have very different themes than a healthcare provider. When establishing roadmaps, you need to indicate the timelines you want to achieve and the order in which you want to implement the themes. For instance, if you're going to implement a customer service automation platform first, you'll want to make sure you prioritise this initiative over others. To automate other functions, they should include in subsequent roadmaps.

Defining and Building structure into your automation

Once you've determined the type of automation you want to implement and the technologies you want to use, it's time to build structure into your automation. You can start by creating automation blueprints that outline the strategies, technologies, and solutions for each department or function. In addition, you can also create an automation governance model that outlines the rules, roles, and responsibilities involved in the overall automation process. Finally, you can create an automation impact assessment model to determine the changes that various business functions need to undergo. By creating these blueprints and models, you'll be able to standardise your automation strategies and easily map them across your organisation. This process will make it much easier to implement and manage your automation initiatives, ultimately leading to success.

Service Automation

A reactive manual remediation process can be costly and disruptive to business, whereas automation can help prevent that disruption. For example, If your company has a significant customer service presence, implementing automation can be a great way to save time and improve customer experience. You can automate customer service functions using several technologies, including artificial intelligence (AI), artificial neural networks, and natural language processing. These technologies can help you automate responses to common questions, change support tickets, and analyse customer data. Another way to implement service automation is to create self-service portals that allow customers to handle their issues and tickets without contacting support personnel. You can also implement workflow automation to streamline the internal customer service processes.

Business process automation

Business process automation is a great way to simplify and standardise your core operations and gain a competitive edge. You can use various technologies to implement business process automation, including artificial intelligence, rule engines, workflow engines, and intelligent workflow systems. These solutions allow you to define and enforce business processes and execute them in real-time. In addition, these solutions will help you integrate your business with other systems and platforms like CRM, ERP, and IT systems. As a result, you can use business process automation to improve customer experience, boost efficiency, and simplify and standardise your business. To do so, you need to create a roadmap that outlines the steps and timelines you want to follow.

By leveraging business process automation, organisations can connect applications and share data across their environment to increase business agility. Another practical example is an enterprise's iPaaS, which allows for fast, accurate integrations. However, time-consuming, error-prone custom integrations can undermine business process automation.

IT process automation

IT process automation is crucial to DevOps transformation and the key to achieving seamless and efficient business and software processes such as Administration and change approval. Before implementing IT process automation, you must identify the appropriate processes and systems to automate. The best way to do this is to create an IT process map that outlines the various processes and their interactions. Once you've identified the processes you want to automate, you can use IT process automation tools to integrate them and make them fully Integrated. When implementing IT process automation, you must remember that you will only see results after some time. There will be a period of adjustment as employees get accustomed to new systems and procedures. That's why you must create a roadmap and timeline for when you want to implement automation. Roadmaps and timelines are the best tools to help you keep track of your progress, identify potential challenges, and stay on track.

Workflow automation

Apologies, readers, for the elaborated section. Workflow automation is the foundation of all the above automation, which we have discusses just ago. Regardless of service automation, Process automation or Business automation, every stage of the process involves workflow. Hence, the knowledge of workflow automation will bear the torch for and redefine our Workflow automation thinking.

What is workflow automation?

Workflow automation uses software to reduce the human input needed for a task. Workflow automation can achieve by defining rules and response actions to trigger specific outcomes under certain conditions, as a result. Workflow automation can apply to various areas – from customer service to sales and marketing. According to research, organisations that use workflow automation are 22% more productive, 17% more accurate, and 25% more profitable than their counterparts.

Why use workflow automation?

Workflow automation can help you drive consistency, save time, and reduce manual errors in your organisation. It would be best if you designed automation to meet your specific needs to get these benefits. With workflow automation, you can drive consistency across your organisation. Workflow Automation can help you standardise and streamline procedures to create a consistent customer experience.

You can track performance against the standard to see if adjustments are needed. In addition, using tools to automate manual tasks can reduce the time required to complete them. As a result, workflow automation can free your team to focus on higher-value activities. When employees have to repeat tasks manually, there is a greater risk of error. With workflow automation, you can reduce these mistakes and improve the accuracy of your results. Lastly, Workflow automation can help you use your resources more effectively by enabling your team to work smarter and more efficiently.

Types of workflow automation

Workflow automation comes in different forms and can apply in various ways. Although all forms of automation have their benefits, each has its limitations. The best workflow automation software supports the majority, if not all, of these types.

Business process automation: This workflow automation uses software to streamline existing business processes. It may also involve modifying or enhancing legacy systems to achieve a better or more consistent business outcome.

Predictive workflow automation: Predictive workflow automation focuses on anticipating needs and triggering actions. It's ideal for situations when events may happen differently than a set schedule. Predictive workflow automation works best when you have an extensive data set to help it learn and respond to specific events and situations.

Hybrid workflow automation: Hybrid workflow automation combines business process and predictive automation. It combines human and machine inputs to deliver the best of both. Hybrid automation can apply to operations where a computer can help make better decisions. However, human judgment is still needed to make the final call. Therefore, hybrid workflow automation often has a computer make suggestions or recommendations, which a human review before making a final decision.

Well, you have beaten! After deep insights into various workflow automation, it's time to learn how to build those.

How to build a workflow automation program?

Creating a workflow automation program starts with evaluating your current operations and identifying areas where automation applies. Once you have your automation strategy, it's time to start building your solutions. First, choose the workflows to automate Before you begin building workflows, you need to identify workflows and processes to automate. This assessment will help you understand how much you can automate. Second, define the automation; After you've identified the workflows, it's time to illustrate the automation. You can do this manually or use existing software to help you design workflows. Third, implement automation. Once your workflow is crafted, it's time to implement it in your organisation further to the approval of various stakeholders. Again, you can do this on your current software or use a workflow management system like Jango or Smartsheet to manage your workflows. Finally, track the automation - After placing your automation, you need to follow it. Tracking the automation progress is crucial because it helps you identify areas where your automation needs improvement.

In a Nutshell, Workflow automation can help you drive consistency, save time, and reduce manual errors in your organisation. Of course, it would help if you designed automation to meet your specific needs to get these benefits. With workflow automation, you can drive consistency across your organisation, save time, reduce manual errors, and improve productivity. To create an automation, you need first to identify workflows and processes to automate. Once you've identified what to automate, it's time to define the automation using software or manually. After the automation is designed, you can implement it in your organisation. Finally, you need to track the automation to see if it needs improvement.

In a Nutshell, Automation is the key to achieving successful DevOps transformation. Organisations must implement automation strategies and technologies that align with their goals and objectives. To do so, you must first understand these automation initiatives' processes and the dreams you want to achieve through them. Once you know your strategy, you can create the themes and roadmaps for your automation initiatives.

Roadmaps will help you prioritise the initiatives that are most crucial and help you achieve your objectives within the correct timeframes. When implementing automation strategies, creating blueprints, establishing structure, and building automation into your business processes are essential. This will allow you to standardise your automation strategies and make them easily scalable across your organisation. As a result, you can transform your business and become a DevOps transformation leader with the right automation strategies and technologies.

CHAPTER 4: A HOLISTIC APPROACH TO CONTINUOUS INTEGRATION

Continuous Integration: Entails developers routinely merge their code changes into a central repository as part of the Continuous software development process.

After a detailed drill-down of structuring your automation, the next immediate DevOps practice that requires deep diving is Continuous Integration, also known as CI. In short, without CI/CD Implementation, DevOps adoption in any organisation will not achieve its mission, as CI/CD is the heart of automation.

Today's businesses must operate at lightning-fast speeds to keep up with the digital economy. To run at a good clip of lightening fast speed, software developers must write code, test it, and release it faster than ever before. Unfortunately, discovering problems in the code after writing it is very expensive and time-consuming. Fortunately, continuous integration (CI) testing can help you catch bugs as early as possible so that you can fix them sooner rather than later. This chapter details Continuous Integration and why it matters for any organisation. It also helps you understand how an organisation can implement CI testing in their software development process and several examples of CI testing. Best practices and Common mistakes to avoid in CI Discipline.

What Is Continuous Integration?

Continuous Integration refers to the practice of testing code frequently. Sometimes people use "continuous delivery" and "continuous deployment" to refer to the same ideas, but they're slightly different practices. The concept behind CI is that every time someone on the development team changes the code, they run a series of tests to ensure that the code works as expected. If the code fails the test, they know there's a problem and can fix it as soon as possible. The idea behind CI is that every time someone on the development team changes the code, they run a series of tests to ensure that the code works as expected. If the code fails the test, the team knows there's a problem and can fix it as soon as possible.

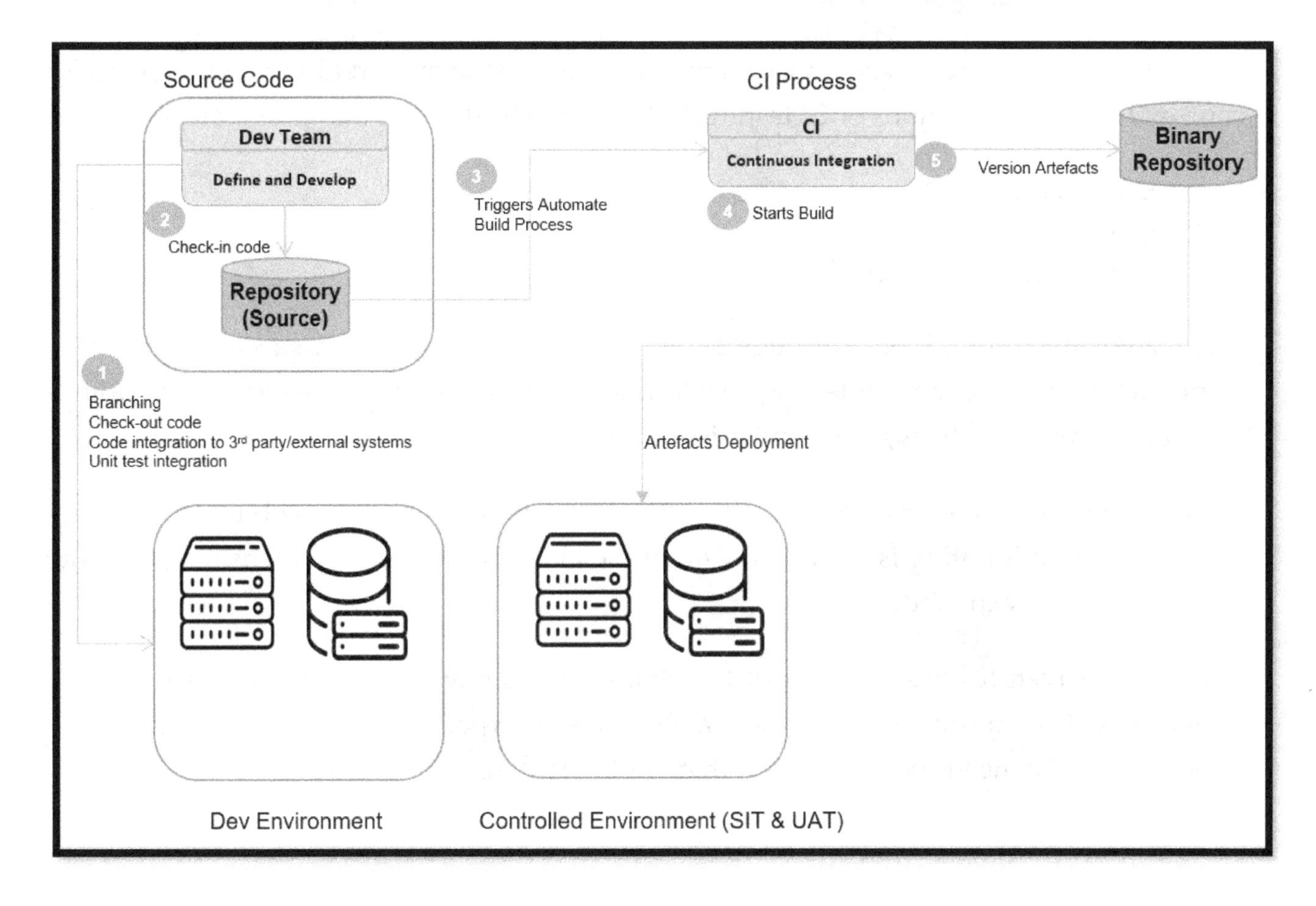

Why Does Continuous Integration Matter?

An organisation can benefit significantly by setting up continuous Integration for the coding practice, including faster software release cycles, better code quality, and fewer bugs. If a CI test fails, the team can fix the problem immediately rather than setting aside time for it later in their cycle. Depending on the type of CI testing that organisation implements, they can also reduce costs by discovering and squashing bugs before they become more significant issues. In addition, it's a great way to ensure that your code meets your company's quality bar.

How to Implement Continuous Integration?

Let's discuss the different types of CI testing you can implement and how to set them up. Of course, there are many kinds of CI testing, but they can be divided into three categories:

1. Static analysis,
2. Unit testing, and
3. Behaviour-driven testing.

Static analysis: testing looks for bugs before the code has even been executed. The most common type of static analysis testing is code analysis. You check for code security, reliability, and quality concerns during code analysis.

Unit testing is when Developer writes small, isolated code designed to test specific functionality. Unit testing is integral to continuous Integration because it ensures that your code performs as expected.

Behaviour-driven testing is a type of test that explores how real users interact with your application. This means you can test for bugs like unexpected user behaviour (i.e., what happens when someone clicks a button that's not meant for them to click?).

CI With Static Analysis

CI with static analysis is the most basic type of CI testing. It can perform by any developer with a basic knowledge of the source code they're working on. You can use it to test the quality of your code and ensure it meets your company's standards. There are many tools you can use to perform static analysis testing. You can also use an IDE (Integrated Development Environment) to check your code for common issues, including:

CI With Unit Tests

Unit tests are small automated tests designed to test the logic of units of code, typically modules or functions. If you're unfamiliar with unit testing, you may have heard it referred to as a "test pyramid." The idea behind a test pyramid is that you should have more unit tests than other types of tests, such as integration tests and system tests. There are many tools available for unit testing. Some of the most popular tools for unit testing include:

CI With Behavior-Driven Tests

Product owners and developers write behaviour-driven tests to test functionality from the user's perspective. Instead of testing every single path of your code, you're only testing the few paths that a user would take through your code. Behaviour-driven tests are typically automated with an end-to-end tool like Selenium or Cucumber. You can also use a code-based approach to testing that automates code execution and performs assertions to check for expected outcomes.

What are all the common Mistakes to avoid in Continuous Integration?

While discussing CI, it is worth zooming in on common mistakes to avoid in CI Implementation. By avoiding mistakes, you can yield the maximum benefits from CI. There are many common mistakes can usually happen in the CI environment. Some of them include

Selecting the wrong tool: While the right tool will make your team's lives more accessible, the wrong tool can be a nightmare.

Need to test more: Some CI tools allow you to configure how often a test is run. While you might want to run your tests frequently, you don't want to run them so often that it's a waste of time.

Testing too often is a waste of time: Not testing the right things - It's essential to test the right parts of your code. You should only test parts of your code that receive a little traffic or don't need to test as often.

Forgetting to set up the right environment for test runs: You need a set of tools to run tests. These tools can run tests in different settings, for example, on Windows, Mac OS X or Linux. However, suppose you're using a Mac or Linux system. You may need a graphical user interface (GUI) application like Xcode to create and manage test environments.

Continuous Integration - Best Practices

By avoiding common mistakes, you have indirectly started practicing the best practices. So let's look at the best practices that can help your Codes into hygiene and health through CI.

Continuous Integration is a great deal for you if you're using it. CI uses the tools to ensure that pieces of code are always verified before merging into your Centralised or Decentralised and other Source Code Management systems.

Practice early, frequent commits: First and foremost is to ensure all the source code, configuration files, scripts, and libraries are in source control toward implementing continuous Integration and tracking every change.

Each commit initiates a series of automated tests to provide immediate feedback on the change. When integrating large, complex changes, committing regularly ensures that the team works on the same foundations, facilitating collaboration and reducing the likelihood of painful merge conflicts.

To reap the benefits of continuous Integration, each Developer must share their changes with the rest of the team by pushing to the main or master branch and updating their working copy to include everyone else's changes. As a general rule, commit to the main or master branch at least once per day.

Regular pushing of changes to the main or master branch can be unsettling for teams used to working in long-running branches. This may be primarily attributable to concern about being judged by others or the task being too sizable to complete.

Creating a team culture that focuses on collaboration is critical. As with any change in work practices, it pays to talk about how you work as a team. Working as a team to break tasks into smaller, discrete pieces can help individuals adopt this practice.

Another alternative is to use feature flags when complex branches host new features that have yet to be released. These allow developers to control the visibility of specific functionality in different environments, enabling code changes to be merged and included in the build for testing while remaining invisible to users.

Leverage Green Build Strategy: The objective is to avoid laying flawed foundations and keep the code up to date. It is much more efficient to address issues as they arise, allowing for a q if something goes wrong in production.

In a parallel development environment, if a build fails, the team's priority is to get it working again. Therefore, it's tempting to blame whoever made the last change and delegate the task of resolving the problem to them. However, blaming the team rarely results in a positive team culture. Furthermore, it is less likely to uncover the root cause of a problem.

You can improve the entire CI/CD process by making it the whole team's responsibility to address a failing build and try to understand what caused the failure. But, of course, when the pressure is on and tensions are high, that is easier said than done; developing a DevOps culture is also an exercise in continuous improvement!

Of course, having to drop everything to fix a failing build, only to discover that it was caused by something trivial - a syntax error or a missed dependency - can be infuriating. To avoid this, team members should build and run an initial set of tests locally before sharing their changes.

Environments Refresh: It's worth refreshing your non-production settings between each production rollout to yield the maximum CI benefits. When your environments run for an extended period, it becomes increasingly challenging more work to keep a trail of all the configuration changes and updates applied to each environment. Therefore, it pays to update settings with your production baseline code version.

Optimisation of pipeline stages: Jobs and steps are contained in CI pipelines. Jobs are the activities that occur within a specific stage. Once all jobs are completed, the code advances to the next stage. Optimise stages so that failures are easy to identify and fix.

Stages are a convenient way to organise similar jobs. However, a few jobs in your pipeline could safely run in an earlier stage and not harm your product if they fail. Consider running these jobs earlier to speed up the CI process.

In a Nutshell, CI is integral to modern software development and can help you produce high-quality code. The best way to implement CI is with static analysis, unit tests, and behaviour-driven tests. You can implement CI by selecting the right tool, avoiding common mistakes, testing the right things, and implementing the best practices. CI is the way to go if you want to improve your software development process. CI offers much, from faster release cycles to better code quality.

CHAPTER 5: A HOLISTIC APPROACH TO CONTINUOUS DEPLOYMENT

Continuous Deployment: Next step of continuous delivery

Continuous Deployment is the technique of releasing software updates to users quickly and frequently. It automates the entire code deployment process to release new code changes seamlessly and frequently without extensive manual testing or a release process. This chapter will examine why continuous Deployment matters, how to implement a Continuous Deployment strategy, and what tools are available to help you get there.

What is Continuous Deployment?

Continuous Deployment automates software releases to environments, including staging and Production, based on feedback from automated testing tools. Continuous Deployment aims to continuously integrate code into a stage or production environment without human intervention. As a result, continuous Deployment is a great way to decrease deployment times and increase your team's productivity. At its core, continuous Deployment is a change management strategy. It changes how teams manage code releases, prioritising speed and automation over manual testing and approval processes. This shift in organisational priorities can help your organisation become more agile.

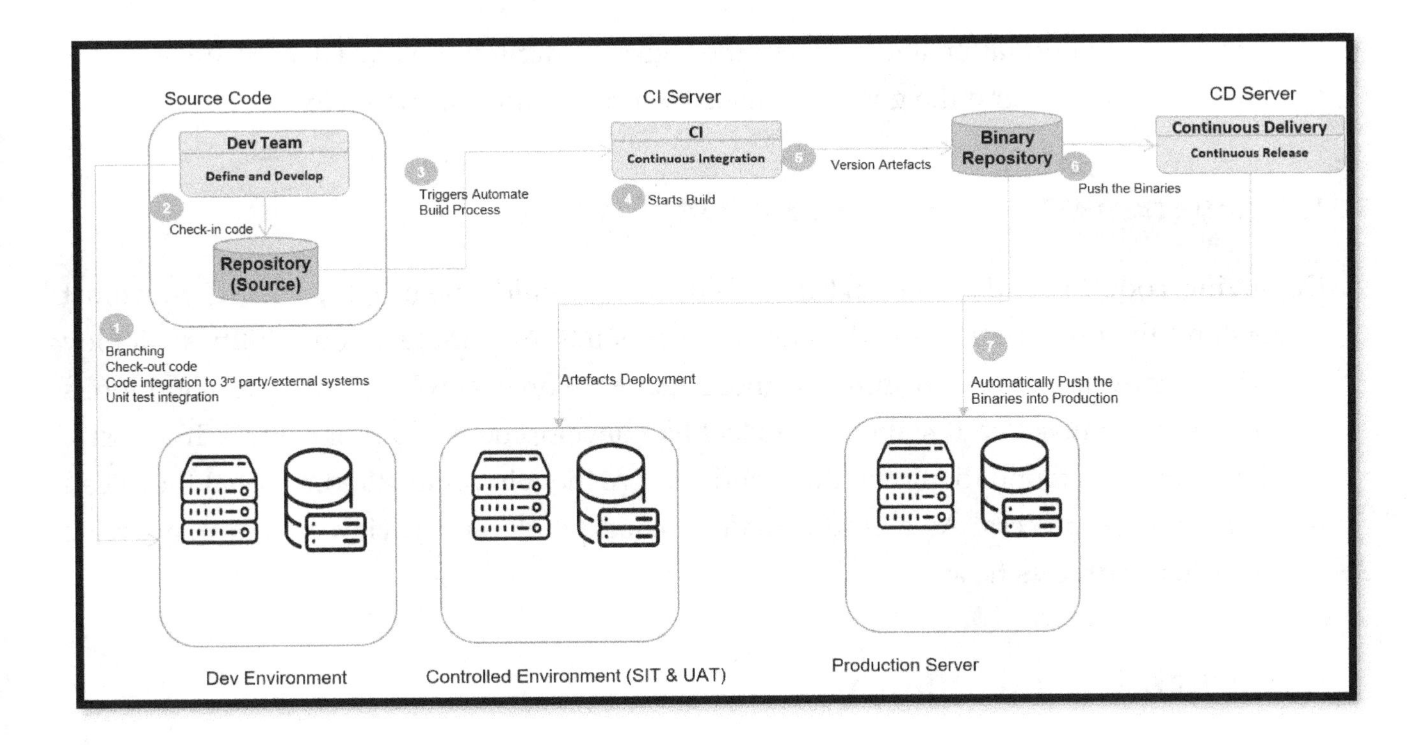

Why Does Continuous Deployment Matter?

If you're already practicing continuous integration, the next step is continuous Deployment. Continuous Deployment means that every change in your codebase gets deployed to your end users. All the testing and approval are automated, so you can push new code to Production anytime. But, of course, you want without waiting for someone else to give you the go-ahead. For software teams, this means having the ability to respond to user feedback immediately instead of being tied up in the approval process for a new release. Also, continuous Deployment helps to create a more reliable product by decreasing the time between when a bug introduces and when it's fixed. Suppose your team can respond to user feedback immediately. In that case, you can decrease the time between when a bug is introduced and when it's fixed. For example, let's say your team must wait a week for approval to deploy a new product version. If a user reports a bug, it'll take a week for the team to get that information and then another week to deploy the fix. This process is called the time to resolution, and the goal is to make the time as short as possible.

Considerations for Continuous Deployment

Deploying code to Production isn't a decision that should make lightly. First, you must understand the organisational and technical factors that may impact your ability to deploy code frequently and work to mitigate those factors. For example, shifting to continuous Deployment can make your stakeholders feel like development is out of control. If you still need to establish a foundation with them and involve them in understanding what they need from the release process. As a result, manual checkpoints and review stages may create latencies in the process flow.

Code stability and quality

Before diving into any automated process, ensure your code is written to a standard that allows for smooth, error-free Deployment. Otherwise, you'll be wasting a lot of time and effort trying to automate the process when the code is the roadblock. In addition, to ensure you have stable code, you'll want to keep a close eye on your code quality metrics. Metrics include test coverage and code complexity.

Automated testing

Automated testing is a crucial piece of the continuous deployment puzzle. The tool tells you when your code is ready for Production and when it's broken. You'll want to ensure you have automated tests in place for both the front and back ends of your product. For front-end code, you'll want to ensure you're testing what your users interact with: the design, user flow and so on. Front-end testing tools like Selenium and Webdriver make this easy. With the help of a tool like Zapier, you can trigger automated front-end tests whenever code pushes to your codebase.

Infrastructure

Ensure your infrastructure can handle the increased deployment frequency. For example, if you're currently deploying code once a month, but the team would like to deploy daily, you'll want to ensure your servers can handle the extra traffic. You'll also want to ensure that everything, including your network connections and code dependencies, is up to date and running smoothly.

Code ownership

It would be best if you also considered who owns the code that is getting deployed. If you're automating the deployment process, who will approve the change? Who will be responsible for the change at each step of the process? If an error occurs, who is responsible for resolving it? Is a single person monitoring all the deployments, or are they being pushed out simultaneously and independently?

Organisational culture and team structure

Finally, you must ensure that the organisational culture and team structure are conducive to continuous Deployment. For example, if your team feels uncomfortable deploying code frequently, there's a good chance they won't do it.

Continuous Deployment Vs Continuous Delivery

Before getting into the nitty-gritty of implementing continuous Deployment, it's important to distinguish between Continuous Deployment and continuous delivery. The two terms are often used interchangeably, but there is a slight difference in their meanings. With continuous delivery, the team is expected to ship the product on demand, no matter the time of the day. On the other hand, continuous Deployment has a set time of the day when the product is deployed to the live environment. In other words, the Deployment is automated but happens at a predefined time.

How to Implement Continuous Deployment

If you've worked through the organisational and technical considerations, you're ready to implement continuous Deployment. You'll want to ensure you have a system for automating your deployments and a staging environment that can receive and process those automated deployments. Deploying to Production To deploy code to Production, it must first deploy into staging. For smaller teams, this staging environment might be the production environment. However, for larger teams, it should be a different environment. Once your code is deployed to staging, you can use automated and manual testing to ensure the release is ready. Once your team is prepared to deploy the code to Production, a single button click will trigger the deployment process.

Tools for Continuous Delivery and Deployment

There are a variety of tools that can help you automate your continuous deployment strategy and make it more efficient. Here are a few of the essential tools:

Source control: Source control is essential to any development process, but if you're trying to implement continuous Deployment, it becomes even more critical. To deploy code to Production, you must have a copy of that code in source control.

Automated testing tools: Automation testing tools inform you when your code is ready for Production. Hence, they are essential to releasing code quickly and frequently.

Deployment tools: Deployment tools like Deployment Bot, Deploy.com, and Octobox make the deployment process seamless. They allow you to deploy code to staging environments with one click and deploy that code to Production with another click. - CI/CD tools -

Continuous integration and continuous delivery tools make it easy to implement continuous Deployment by automating your workflow.

Common Mistakes of Continuous Deployment Implementation

While continuous Deployment is, by nature, a continuous process, it's helpful to think of the implementation as a series of discrete steps. These steps will help ensure that you get all the critical components of your implementation and that you're prepared for any hiccups along the way.

Code stability and quality: Your entire implementation relies on the stability of your code. If the code is stable, you can deploy it smoothly, and your execution will succeed.

Automated testing: Quality automated testing is foundational to successful continuous Deployment. Before deploying code, you must have confidence that the testing will pass.

Infrastructure: Your infrastructure must be ready to handle the increased traffic that comes with continuous Deployment to ensure your implementation is successful.

Deployment to Production: You must be able to deploy to a staging environment before you can deploy to Production. If you skip this step, you risk deploying broken code to Production and causing significant damage.

CHAPTER 6: CONTINUOUS DELIVERY COMPANION

Continuous Delivery: The capability to quickly implement modifications, new features, configurations, issue fixes, and experiments into production.

With the rise of DevOps and digital transformation, businesses have increasingly focused on releasing software faster. In doing so, they have introduced concepts such as Continuous Integration, Continuous Delivery, and DevOps. These techniques accelerate software development and release processes, making new features available to users more quickly. However, an organisation still needs to implement these approaches. In that case, you will likely need to decide which one (or more) would be the most beneficial for your business moving forward. Read on for an introduction to Continuous Delivery and five ways to make it work for your business.

What is Continuous Delivery?

Continuous Delivery (or CD) is a software release approach that emphasise increasing automation and testing to minimise risk and increase velocity. It is an evolution of CI/CD that aims to streamline the release process and increase the number of deployments per day. In a nutshell, the CD is the process of automating the build, test, and deployment of code to deliver software faster and more reliably. To excel at CD, you must have a strategy for ensuring that build, test, and deployment processes are consistent and reliable. In a nutshell, the goal of continuous delivery is to have a fully automated deployment pipeline that can measure in hours and minutes, not days. Companies focus on making their delivery process repeatable and predictable to achieve that goal. They also emphasise the need for automation and reliable testing so that teams know that what they're releasing is ready to go.

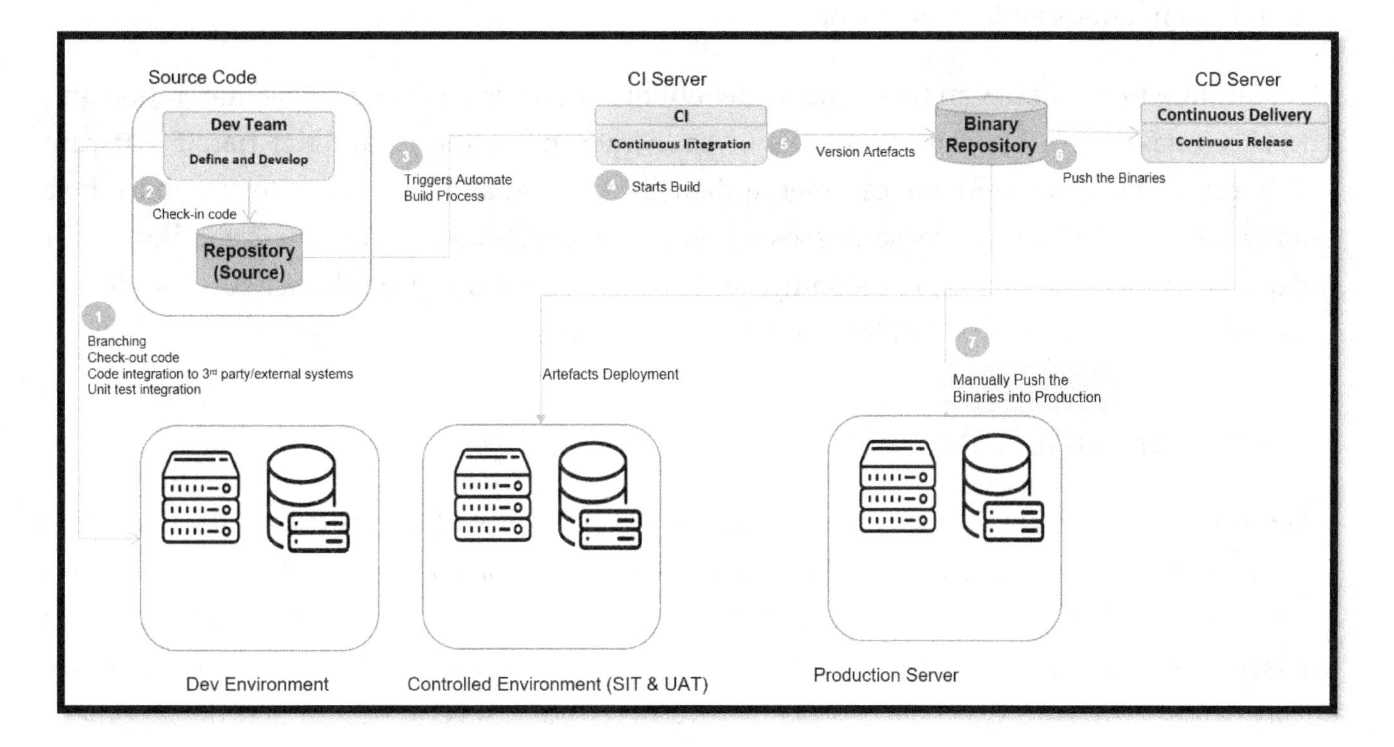

What are the Benefits of Continuous Delivery?

Continuous Delivery is loaded with dozens of benefits. Let us name a few below

Releases with low Risk: Continuous delivery's main objective is to make software deployments simple, low-risk processes that may be carried out whenever needed. Establishing zero-downtime deployments invisible to users is relatively simple by implementing patterns like blue-green deployments.

Higher-quality product Release: Teams may concentrate on user research and higher-level testing activities like unit tests, acceptance tests, performance testing, and vulnerability scans when developers have automated tools to find regressions within minutes. Continuously constructing a deployment pipeline during the delivery process ensures that quality is ingrained in goods and services from the start.

Faster time to market: is an unavoidable benefit of Continuous Delivery. The integration and test/fix phases can take several weeks or even months in the traditional tiered software delivery lifecycle. Developers can merge their integration and regression testing into their daily work and eliminate these phases when teams collaborate to automate the build and deployment, environment provisioning, and regression testing procedures. We also do not have the extensive rework that the staged approach does.

Common Pitfalls of Continuous Delivery

While CD can be highly beneficial, it's essential to be mindful of any pitfalls that could arise. Here are a few common issues you should consider when considering CD. First, building too much automation too early. One of the biggest challenges with implementing CD is creating a large amount of automation too early in the process. That can be challenging because you may only know your exact needs once you've undergone several design and development iterations. If you build too much automation too early, you may be stuck with a rigid process for the long term that doesn't fit the needs of your organisation. Many companies prefer implementing an approach like Lean Delivery instead of CD. Automation not being built by developers - Another pitfall of continuous delivery is that the automation is not driven by the developers but by other IT teams. This can create issues because the team responsible for automation needs to be in the trenches of the development process and, therefore, might need to be made aware of potential problems along the way.

Enable Continuous Delivery with Automation

Another vital factor to consider when implementing CD is ensuring that your automation is working correctly and is ready to handle the volume of work coming through the system. For example, suppose you're using a continuous integration platform such as TeamCity, Jenkins, or Travis CI. In that case, you'll want to ensure that it's integrated with version control systems such as Git with a test suite. That can run every time someone pushes code to your repository. You'll also want to ensure that the build process can handle the number of test cases you need to run since you'll run them automatically each time code is added to version control.

Create a reliable test environment

Another issue with continuous delivery is that your test environment needs to be more reliable. If you're implementing automated testing, you will likely run those tests against a test environment. It would be best to ensure that that environment is reliable and consistent so that your testing will accurately reflect how your software performs in the real world. Consider creating multiple test environments to run numerous tests in parallel. This will take some organisational effort, but it will allow you to run tests more quickly.

Continuously Deliver Software with a Staged Rollout

Another critical aspect of CD is continuously delivering software with a staged rollout. While you are automating the process of releasing software, you are also continuously testing that software. Ensure that it performs as expected and has no bugs or issues. This will allow you to identify and fix any problems before you push your software out to a broader audience. When you're continuously delivering, you'll want to ensure that each stage of the deployment process is also automated. Staged rollouts will help ensure that the process remains consistent and that you constantly deploy from a tested software version.

Organise your Infrastructure and Code Together

Another critical factor to consider when implementing CD is that you should be Organising your infrastructure and code together. It would help if you stored your code in the same repository as the configuration and instructions for running that code in production. Keeping your code and infrastructure files in the same repository is crucial because all the information you need to deploy code will be in your repository. You will be able to see who made the changes and when. You will also see what else is in the same repository as your code. Organising your infrastructure and code together can be extremely helpful when troubleshooting issues or tracking down bottlenecks in your deployment process.

Train your Developers to be Testers

Another way to ensure that you continuously deliver high-quality software is to train your developers to be testers. You expect them to write and execute test cases for their code. Turning them into testers will allow them to identify inconsistencies and bugs in their code before anyone else can use it. It will also enable them to ensure that their code is performing as expected and that it serves the task that it is intended to achieve. This will also help them identify potential issues with their test cases since they will be actively using the code as it's being written. Finally, this will help them to identify areas where their code might need to be improved or fixed.

Establish a quality control process

Another way to ensure that your software is high-quality and ready to be released is to establish a quality control process. For example, you will have a group of people or a team reviewing the software being released to ensure that it's ready to be used by the wider audience. This is important because you want to avoid releasing buggy software that has issues that cause problems for your users. It also helps to prevent new features from being accidentally broken as more code is added to the application. You can achieve this by creating a quality control board that reviews code before it's released. Consider implementing a feature freeze period where a specific team or group reviews all new code before it is added to the application.

Make your software delivery process transparent.

Another way to ensure that your software delivery process is transparent is to make it visible to your team. You can accomplish this by displaying the state of each item being worked on in your backlog in a single tool that all your team members can access. This will allow everyone to see their work status and ensure that everything runs smoothly with all items in the backlog. This will also let everyone see when their work is ready to be reviewed so that everything is predictable when it comes time for them to show their work to the rest of the team. This transparency will help your team be more accountable and ensure that work is progressing as it should.

At its core, continuous delivery is about ensuring you release high-quality software more frequently. To do that, you need to ensure that your team follows a set of best practices that will allow them to deliver that software more efficiently and effectively. That means ensuring your team members pursue a consistent process and work effectively together. And ensuring they have everything they need to perform their work well. It also means ensuring that the software you deliver is free of defects and ready to be used by your end users.

CHAPTER 7: CONTINUOUS TESTING

Continuous Testing: Execution of automated tests as part of the software delivery pipeline in order to get immediate feedback on various risks

DevOps adoption comes with many Continual practices, such as Continuous Integration, Continuous Deployment, and Continuous Delivery. Some experts believe that CI/CD is sufficient to manage DevOps adoption. But unfortunately, we must look around at other continuous processes, namely, Continuous Testing and Continuous Code scanning.

Even a non-specialist can agree that Continuous Testing and Test Automation are essential for developing high-quality software and providing timely feedback on the impact of changes.

What is Continuous Testing?

Continuous testing is a practice in DevOps automation that aims to improve the quality of our code by detecting if it has broken due to a change. Continuous Testing shows code regression immediately after making a change and before moving on to the next task. This way, we ensure that every commit to our codebase is high quality, with minimal risk of introducing bugs or breaking existing functionality. Test automation is designing automated tests that can run repeatedly and independently from a human tester. With test automation in place, any future changes or additions will discover quickly and easily, which reduces maintenance time and cost for your organisation.

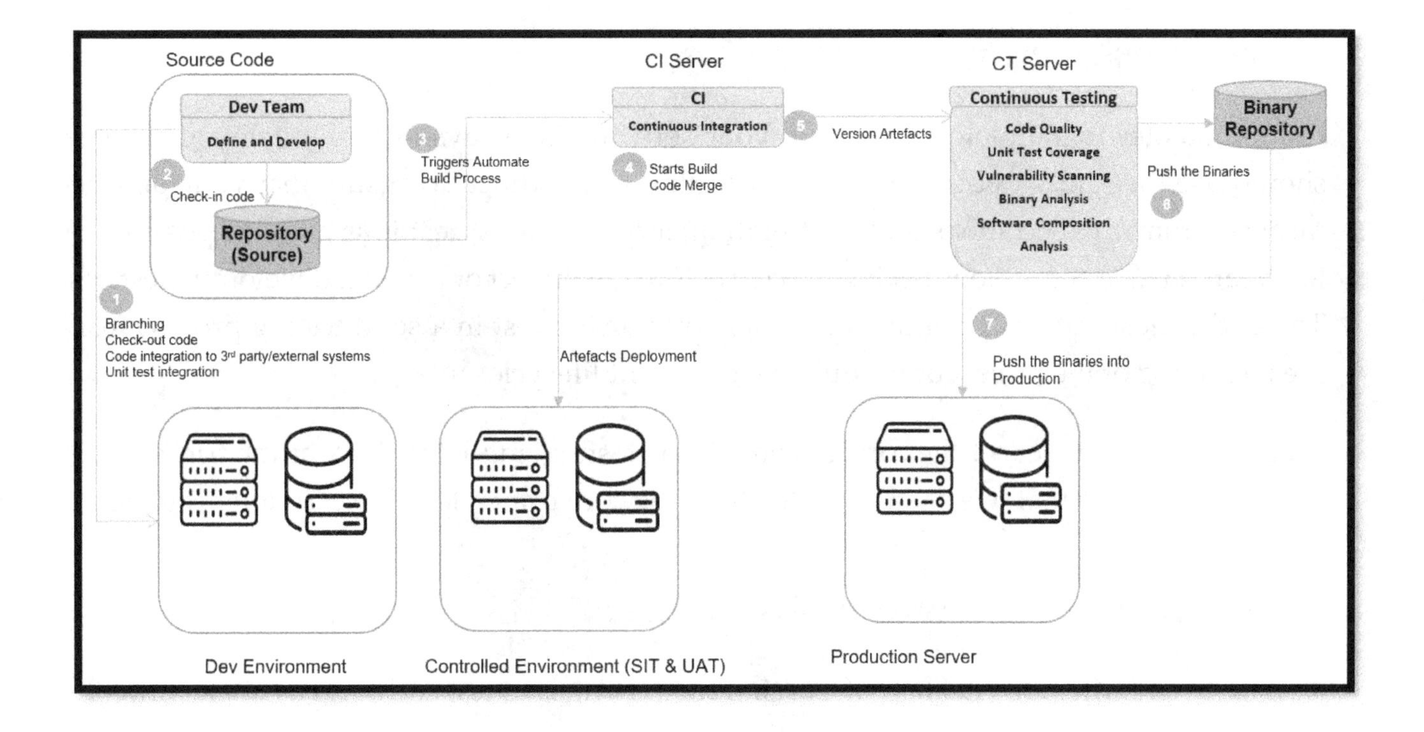

Why is continuous testing necessary?

Automated tests are crucial for ensuring the quality of the software. However, they are time-consuming and require significant resources to develop. As a result, many software teams must prioritise testing only after the product is built. The problem is that manual testing is time-consuming, expensive, prone to human error, and cannot detect regressions. As a result, we will often only be able to find bugs once the product is almost finished. Any changes will require the entire product or parts to be re-tested. In addition, if we want to add new features or make changes to the product, we must keep existing functionality intact. This behaviour leads to the risk of building less reliable and less secure software, which can negatively impact customer satisfaction and company reputation.

When to use continuous testing?

Continuous testing aims to ensure that your software is always of high quality. The team should use the same process and tools for testing and coding. To ensure that your product meets customer expectations and is of high quality, you must test it as early as possible. A team can set up a continuous testing process before the project or product development starts. To get the most out of Continuous Testing, you must invest in a solid testing process from the beginning of the project or product development lifecycle.

Well, we have now learnt the rope of continuous testing and let us look at the tricks of the trades. But, before that, we need to understand the core principles of Continuous Testing.

Core Principles of Continuous Testing

Test early and often: A vital part of Continuous Testing is to test early and as often. Since the objective is to catch bugs early, we need to test the code as soon as possible when they are easier to fix. As a result, we can ensure that our product works as expected and address issues before they become significant problems.

Verify the Build: The "verify the build" principle means that every time we change the code, we want to ensure that it is building without any errors.

Verify the code works correctly: The next step after verifying the build is to test the code to ensure it works correctly.

Manage the risk of breaking the product: As soon as we have verified the build and the code works correctly, we need to ensure that we don't break anything.

Verify the build after every change: After we have verified the build and code, we must go back and re-verify the build to ensure that it continues to build successfully after each change.

What is the role of Continuous Testing in Test automation?

We can implement automated tests for key functionality as part of a continuous build and test process. Automated tests are crucial for reducing variability and increasing the speed at which we can identify issues. For example, you can use automated tests to check that your most vital functionality works correctly after every change. This way, you will be able to discover issues quickly and identify them before they become significant problems. Automated test cases can also use to define and verify product requirements. This way, you can ensure that your team will build the right product.

The benefits of Continuous Testing

Increased Quality: By continuously testing the product, you can reduce the time it takes to find issues, which means that you will find them earlier, and they will be easier to fix. This will ensure that the quality of the product is significantly higher than if we were to do manual testing.

Reduced Time to Market: A continuous testing process with automated tests will reduce the time it takes to develop a product. Continuous Testing will help you reduce the time to market, which is vital for many companies.

Increased Productivity: By continuously testing the code, you can discover issues early and quickly fix them before moving on to the next task. Doing this will make it easier for teams to focus on completing their tasks.

Reduced Risk: Continuous testing will help reduce the risk of delivering a faulty product after various rounds of testing and multiple iterations of test case execution.

How to practice Continuous testing?

Set up an Automated Continuous Integration Pipeline: Invest in setting up an automated continuous integration pipeline from the beginning of your project or product development as part of DevOps adoption. This will make it easier to implement continuous testing later on.

Identify potential Issues: Start by identifying potential issues in your code. Then, you can run static code analysis and review your code for possible bugs before testing.

Automated Tests: Once you have identified potential issues in your code, you can implement automated tests. Automated tests will let you know if there are issues in your code and make it possible to fix them before they cause problems.

Fix Issues immediately: Whenever you find issues in your code, you must fix them immediately. This way, you can ensure that any changes don't cause disruptions in your code.

Ensure that each Commit is of High Quality: As soon as you change your code, run a build, and automatically test it to ensure the new change breaks no functionality.

Ensure every change isn't Breaking the product: You can also use continuous testing to ensure that every change isn't breaking the product. This way, you can ensure you don't introduce bugs when fixing issues.

Build a regression test pipeline: After setting up an automated build, test, and integration process, you must place a system to test the software. You can do this by setting up a regression test pipeline, where each pipeline stage is responsible for testing a specific part of your product. The regression test pipeline will let you ensure that your product works correctly after each change and catch issues as early as possible.

Automated UI Tests

UI tests are designed to check the functionality of your application in a natural, simulated environment. They are like end-to-end tests but focused on the user interface instead of the entire application. A UI test includes the creation of an application, execution of the test, and the monitoring of the test results. UI tests are instrumental when you want to test an app on multiple devices and browsers. You can also use them to check user interaction and ensure that your application works as expected. Finally, UI tests are often part of an automated regression test pipeline. You can use them to run simulations, like filling out a form or clicking a button. UI test automation helps you identify issues and ensure that changes to the application don't break any functionality.

Automated API Tests

API tests are designed to test your application from the inside out. They are the best way to test your application's backend and ensure that the changes made to other parts of the product don't break the back end. API tests are great for creating a stable and reliable back end for your product. They are also helpful for testing different scenarios and verifying that your application works correctly. Like other automated tests, API tests can be part of a continuous integration test pipeline. You can use them to test your application's functional and non-functional features, including code paths and parameters.

In a Nutshell, Continuous testing is crucial for building quality into our software and ensuring that we don't break any functionality when making changes. The key to Continuous Testing is ensuring we integrate testing into the entire development process. We must test as quickly as possible before moving to the next task. To get the most out of Continuous Testing, we need to invest in setting up a solid automated test process right from the start of the project. Remember that the automatic testing process will make it easier to implement continuous testing. And ensure our product is high quality as part of your DevOps transformation. Hence, take advantage of the Continuous Testing principle to avoid inflating the cost of poor quality.

CHAPTER 8: CONTINUOUS CODE SCANNING

Continuous Code Scanning: Constantly scan the code for bugs, quality, technical debts, security flaws, and code smells.

Software Security is critical in DevOps, continuous integration (CI), and continuous code inspection (CCI) processes. You must wait until the testing phase to catch the security defects in these fast-paced development cycles. You must continuously inspect your code and catch anomalies as soon as they appear. Operational efficiency is a crucial goal of DevOps, CI, and CCI processes. The sooner you can identify issues with your application and make corrections before deployment. The more time you have for other activities like testing or releasing new features into production. Here are some best practices for using Continuous Security scanning tools to catch defects early and prevent them from reaching your users. This is often called DevSecOps in the industry. DevSecOps is nothing but where DevOps meets Continuous Security.

Before diving deep into this chapter, the readers should remember the golden rules.

"SECURITY IS EVERYONE ACCOUNTABILITY"

What is Application Security Testing?

Application security testing (AST) is the practice of investigating the security of application software products. It includes finding existing vulnerabilities and the potential for future vulnerabilities in an application's code or design. Application security testing covers software's functionality, usability, and reliability; the confidentiality, integrity, and availability of data. The compliance of software with applicable laws and regulations; and the application's capacity to fulfil the business process for which it was intended. AST is a subset of the broader security testing group of activities. Those activities may include penetration testing, external and internal audits, social engineering, etc. The primary goal of AST is to identify potential security risks with the software through code reviews, static analysis, and dynamic analysis. Let's glance thru the different types of security testing.

Why is Application Security Testing Important in DevOps?

Testing for security vulnerabilities is critical to application development and must begin early. However, with DevOps, Continuous Integration (CI) and Continuous Code Inspection (CCI) processes, you can't wait until the testing phase to catch defects. Instead, you need to continuously inspect your code as it's being written and get immediate feedback. For example, suppose your code is being automatically tested for security vulnerabilities. Then, detect and correct the issues with the early code change instead of waiting until the final testing phase when there is a higher risk of introducing new defects while fixing others.

What is Dynamic Application Security Testing?

Dynamic application security testing (DAST) is the process of testing application software for potential security vulnerabilities during execution. The goal is to find security flaws that would otherwise remain hidden until the software is put into production. A DAST tool monitors an application's input and output to look for signs of malicious activity. It also analyses the code to look for vulnerabilities that hackers could exploit. Dynamic application security testing is often automated, using tools that simulate real-life application environments, such as a browser or mobile application. This application testing must occur during the DevOps, continuous integration (CI), and continuous code inspection (CCI) processes because it takes place while the application is running rather than after it has been compiled.

What is Static Application Security Testing?

Static application security testing (SAST) is the process of reviewing the code of an application for potential security vulnerabilities. The goal is to find defects in the application's source code that could cause the application to fail or put confidential data at risk of being stolen. SAST is a manual process performed by a software engineer who analyses the application's code for security weaknesses. As with DAST, a SAST tool can help identify specific areas of concern in the code. While SAST primarily reviews the code, a tool can help automate the process, particularly in large-scale software projects.

What is Binary Analysis and Software Composition Analysis?

Binary analysis and software composition analysis (BC/SCA) tools evaluate the parts of an application, like the libraries and modules it uses, during the build phase. They are used to understand the application's dependencies, including third-party code libraries, and assess the risk associated with each. Binary analysis tools look at the source code of each software library or module an application uses to determine its risk level. Software composition analysis tools take a deeper analysis of the application's binary code to identify potential security issues derived from the third-party code. BC/SCA tools can help you identify security issues in your application code, particularly third-party code libraries. When you integrate third-party code into your application, such as open-source libraries or modules, you're relying on the security of that code. A BC/SCA tool can help you understand the risk associated with each library and decide if the risk is worth it.

Well, you are aware of different types of security testing. Another question that might arise in your brain is how these testing methods work. What standards are they using? No worries. The following segments will elucidate your questions.

What are OWSAP, CVE and (CWE)?

Open Web Application Security Project (OWASP) is an open-source community focused on improving the security of application software. OWASP publishes a list of the top 10 most critical web application security risks and provides resources to help organisations address them. In addition, OWASP publishes the Common Vulnerability Enumeration (CVE) as a list of common names for published vulnerabilities. Common Vulnerability and Exposures (CWE) is a standardised list of weaknesses that can lead to security breaches. Organisations can use these resources to determine the risk level of third-party code libraries in their applications.

How CVE works?

The MITRE corporation oversees the CVE programme, funded by the Cybersecurity and Infrastructure Security Agency (CISA), which is part of the United States Department of Homeland Security.

CVE entries are concise. They lack technical data and information about risks, impacts, and fixes. You can also find these details in other databases, such as the US National Vulnerability Database (NVD), the CERT/CC Vulnerability Notes Database, and various vendor and other organisation lists.

CVE IDs provide users with a reliable way to identify unique vulnerabilities and coordinate the development of security tools and solutions across these various systems. The MITRE

Corporation maintains the CVE List, but organisations and open-source community members frequently submit security flaws that become CVE entries.

How to have Secure Coding by Continuously Review Changes in Your Repository?

Once you have your code inspection tools set up, you should continuously review the results of their code analysis. In a DevOps environment, this means checking code as it's being added to a code-review repository, like GitHub. Continuously monitoring the changes in this repository enables you to address issues as they arise instead of waiting for a team meeting. As issues are identified, you can correct them immediately before they become a problem. You can also follow up with the responsible engineers to understand the reasoning behind the changes. This review process helps you catch defects as they occur, so they don't make it into the main or master branch.

In a Nutshell, by following these best practices and incorporating security code scanning as part of your Continuous Integration, you can catch defects in your code as they occur. And, you can prevent them from making it into the main or main branch. You can also follow up with engineers to understand the reasoning behind the changes, allowing you to make changes before they become a problem. While application security testing is critical, only some techniques can ensure perfect code. To prevent defects from entering the code in the first place, you must also engage in proper code design, development, and deployment practices.

CHAPTER 9: INFRASTRUCTURE AS CODE

Infrastructure as code: DevOps technique and refactoring with a descriptive model for infrastructure definition and deployment

DevOps is a set of practices and principles that enables organisations to accelerate software deployments. At the same time, Infrastructure as Code (IaC) is a software development methodology that defines and manages the data centre using machine-readable language. IaC is an infrastructure design, deployment, and management approach that treats the data centre as a collection of abstractions rather than physical machines. As a result, we can use IaC in any environment where you can deploy code and provision resources.

This chapter discusses the benefits of adopting DevOps using infrastructure as Code. If you've adopted DevOps, you've probably automated your deployment pipeline using CI/CD. The next logical step is to adopt infrastructure as Code (IAC) so that your Code is used to provision your virtual machines and other infrastructure elements instead of manual processes.

Read on to learn more about the benefits of adopting DevOps with IAC, including reducing the time it takes to rebuild servers from source code, improving security by eliminating manual tasks, and streamlining hybrid cloud deployments.

Before a wholesale look at Infrastructure as Code, it's worth looking at the problems of the Traditional IT model.

The Problems with Traditional IT

Traditional IT infrastructure management is not the best way to keep up with the needs of the current era. With old-school data centres, it is not easy to manage, upgrade and maintain all the equipment. The traditional IT infrastructure also needs to provide a better customer experience.

IT departments are looking for new ways to manage their data centres to provide a better customer experience and keep up with current trends.

What is Infrastructure as Code?

Infrastructure as Code is a process where you use source code to automate the creation and management of infrastructure. Using IAC, you would typically use a source code management system (SCM) such as Git to manage the deployment of your virtual machines. And other infrastructure elements instead of manual processes. If you've automated your deployment pipeline using CI/CD, then adopting IAC is the next logical step in adopting DevOps. With IAC, your Code is used to provision virtual machines and other infrastructure elements instead of manual processes. IAC is a great way to remove ambiguity and avoid mistakes when deploying infrastructure. IAC is especially useful for organisations that want to adopt a hybrid cloud environment. Hybrid cloud deployments require manual work to manage different cloud resources and on-premises infrastructure. You can reduce the risk of human error with IAC. You can also streamline adding new servers to your environment by configuring code items and triggering the deployment through Code.

How does IaC Help DevOps adoption?

Adopting DevOps requires a significant cultural shift, but it provides several benefits that outweigh the costs. Infrastructure as Code (IAC) plays a crucial role in helping organisations adopt DevOps. If you use IAC, you can eliminate the bottlenecks that can occur in manual processes. Manual tasks such as creating virtual machine images, configuring network elements, and setting up load balancers can cause delays in the deployment pipeline. IAC helps you eliminate these bottlenecks. Using IAC to provision infrastructure elements can dramatically reduce the time it takes to rebuild servers from source code. You can eliminate the need for manual tasks that slow down deployments and create inconsistency across different environments. Using VCS to manage your IAC can also help you improve collaboration because multiple individuals can collaborate on a single source code repository. You can create branches in your repository to operate different software versions and use pull requests to review code changes before merging them into the master branch. You can also use VCS to track changes made to your infrastructure elements.

Let us look at the benefits of Iac in Detail.

Reduce the time it takes to rebuild servers from source code

Source code management is the cornerstone of any DevOps initiative. When developers source code manages their applications, they create a single source of truth for all application components, including infrastructure elements such as servers and load balancers. What this means is that all your infrastructure elements are stored in a single master repository. So, Infrastructure Developers or Developers can use the repository to create new virtual machines or scale current servers if necessary. Usually, repositories eliminate the need to store your infrastructure elements in separate locations that need to be manually synchronised to create consistent environments. In addition, with source code management, you can create virtual machines from source code using IAC. This process allows you to create virtual machines with consistent configurations based on source code changes instead of manually configuring servers. In this fashion, the servers created from the source code will have the same operating system, installed software, and configuration settings.

How to Avoid manual configuration to enforce consistency using Iac?

Imagine that you have two teams responsible for building web servers — a DevOps team that manages existing servers and a web development team that creates new servers. Unfortunately, there's no way to know if the configuration settings on these servers are the same unless you manually configure each server. This means that the configuration settings could differ across environments, creating potential issues and impacting application performance. A better solution is to use IAC to create virtual machines from source code and automatically configure each server. This manner helps you to enforce consistency across environments and provide a single source of truth for configuration settings. In addition, using IAC to trigger the deployment of new servers from the source code allows you to quickly scale your application and provision additional capacity in minutes. Your business will thank the IT Unit for saving time.

Improve security by eliminating manual tasks

Manually configuring server security settings can be complicated, especially for organisations that have many servers. Moreover, complex processes can always lead to inconsistencies and false positives, which can unnecessarily add security alerts to your environment. As a result, the specialists and engineers need to spend a whopping of energy there as security is the immediate need of attention in many organisations.

Using IAC to configure server security settings automatically can help you eliminate manual tasks and reduce false positives. You can use IAC to configure security settings on servers and network elements, including firewalls, load balancers, and virtual network environments, which include setting up security groups, network access control lists, and virtual private networks. You can also use IAC to perform security compliance audits and configuration checks to identify potential issues.

Streamline hybrid cloud deployments

Suppose your organisation wants to adopt a hybrid cloud architecture. In that case, you need to find a way to simplify the process of managing different cloud resources and on-premises infrastructure. Infrastructure as Code can help you manage hybrid cloud infrastructure more efficiently, primarily if you use a single SCM to manage both on-premises and cloud resources. Using a single SCM to manage both on-premises and cloud resources allows you to transfer workloads between environments quickly. You can configure and trigger the deployment of virtual machines and other resources from the same source code repository. This streamlined approach allows you to easily manage your hybrid cloud environment and identify changes that need to deploy across environments and domains.

In a Nutshell, Adopting DevOps requires a significant cultural shift. However, it provides several benefits that outweigh the costs. Infrastructure as Code (IAC) is crucial in helping organisations adopt DevOps. Using IAC, you can eliminate the bottlenecks that occur in manual processes and simplify hybrid cloud deployments by using a single SCM to manage both on-premises and cloud resources.

CHAPTER 10: CAPABILITY MODEL AND CAPABILITY SCANNING

Capability model: This is a technique for representing an organisation's business and technology anchor model independent of the structure, processes, people, or domains of the organisation.

DevOps is a culture, not just a set of tools or practices. As the demand for faster software development and release cycles grows, this approach has become increasingly popular. So before stepping into this culture, any aspiring organisation needs to embark on this journey couple of top-focus things to perform without fail. One of them is building a capability model and capability quick scan. Unfortunately, some miss out on these steps and choose the easy ones. This chapter will enlighten you on essential topics such as Technology readiness assessment (TRA), CMM and much more.

Now, look at the basics of what is the Capability maturity model.

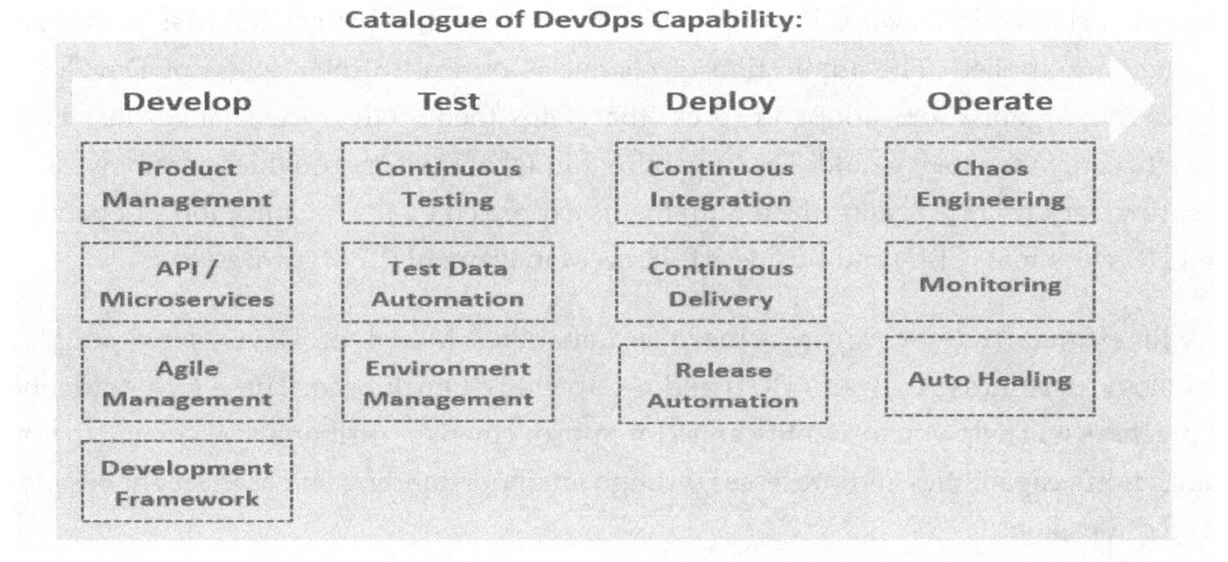

Capability maturity models assess an Organisation's readiness to adopt DevOps practices. In addition, they help identify potential areas of improvement and which process changes are required to adopt DevOps successfully in your organisation. We will discuss how you can achieve a Capability Model of DevOps by adopting the Technology Readiness Analysis (TRA) and a Capability Quick Scan.

Now it's time to introduce the Capability model of DevOps!

Introduction to the Capability Model of DevOps

A Capability Model of DevOps is an organisational model that highlights areas of strength and improvement to chart the journey toward implementing a transformation toward a high-performing, DevOps-oriented organisation. It shows what is needed to achieve the desired maturity level and provides a structure for measuring progress. A Capability Model of DevOps will help organisations to identify and prioritise the areas for improvement and determine which process changes are required to adopt DevOps successfully.

Adopting a change in DevOps is not just about adopting the changes themselves but also how they are applied. The application of change is critical to the success of DevOps. It requires that organisations adopt a process that helps them deliver the changes faster and more efficiently than they would. The Capability Model of DevOps provides a framework for measuring performance against the requirements expressed by the organisation's Capability-based Development (CBD) and Business Process Management (BPM) processes.

We will examine how you can achieve a Capability Model of DevOps by adopting Technology Readiness Analysis (TRA) and a Capability Quick Scan. These two guidelines and practices will help you to identify areas for improvement or further improvement in your organisation's capabilities and processes through an understanding and assessment based on several dimensions:

Technology readiness: This is essential because it measures how well your organisation can rapidly acquire new technology while ensuring that it meets business needs. As part of the Capability-Based Development strategy, the organisation must ensure that all its processes align with its business requirements, which means that all its processes must be consistent. In addition, all stakeholders must agree on their expectations for using new technology. That way, organisations have a clear vision of what they need from their applications.

Capability readiness: This framework helps organisations identify their current readiness for adopting new technologies.

Capability readiness is the capability of an organisation to adopt and utilise new technology. It is a framework that helps organisations identify their current readiness for adopting new technologies. The capability Readiness (C-R) framework has four levels starting from level 1, where the organisation has no current adoption or utilisation of new technology. And level 4, where the organisation has mastered new technology, leads to high-performance levels.

Capability Quick Scan: What and Why?

A Capability Quick Scan is a tool that can be used to assess the state of readiness of an organisation's team and toolset. It processes quickly and easily for implementing DevOps practices. The Capability Quick Scan is built on the Technology Readiness Analysis (TRA) foundation. The Capability Quick Scan's main objective is to assess an organisation's readiness to adopt DevOps practices. To do this, you need to understand the current state, identify areas of improvement, and prioritise them. The Capability Quick Scan will also help you know which process changes are required to adopt DevOps successfully. The data collected will also provide insight into where to focus your efforts and highlight areas that may require investments.

Adopting the Capability Model of DevOps through Capability-based Development (CBD) and Business Process Management (BPM) processes.

Organisations can use The Technology Readiness Analysis (TRA) process to identify potential areas for improvement in productivity, efficiency, and risk management. TRA is an effective tool that helps organisations to identify the areas for improvement and take necessary corrective actions to improve productivity, efficiency, and risk management. The CAPA process is a collection of tools that help you develop a Capability Model of DevOps through TRA. The CAPA processes are designed to help you evaluate the impact of your changes on business performance and determine requirements for improvements to achieve the desired maturity level.

Reviewing the Technology Readiness Analysis Process

This section will review how technology readiness analysis is performed using the Capability Model of DevOps (CMD) tool and the CAPA (Corrective Action Preventive Action) tool. The CMD tool analyses how your Organisation's technologies can adapt to meet business needs. By providing you with a list of capabilities that can apply across your entire organisation and team members' roles within your company or department.

In addition, CMD provides an understanding as to why certain technologies may not work well with certain other technologies in your company or department. The CAPA tool offers insight as to why certain technologies may not work well with others in your organisation and makes recommendations on which changes should be made based on

What is a Technology Readiness Analysis?

The TRA is a methodology that groups tools, cultures, people, processes, and domains based on their evolution and maturity in the industry. It is a tool for assessing the current state of an organisation and prioritising areas for improvement. The concept behind the TRA is like conducting an audit. For the audit, you need to ask the right questions to understand the organisation's current state and recommend improvements that will help it reach the desired state. The TRA includes the following generic questions:

1. What is the current state of your organisation?
2. What is your desired state?
3. What are the gaps?
4. What is the recommended action?

How to Achieve the Capability Model of DevOps using TRA and Capability Quick Scan?

The recommended approach for achieving a Capability Model of DevOps is as follows:

1. First, conduct a Technology Readiness Analysis.
2. Identify the gaps.
3. Conduct a Capability Quick Scan.
4. Prioritise the gaps and recommend actions.
5. Put the recommended actions in place and
6. Measure the impact.

Limitations of the current approach and conclusion

A Capability Model of DevOps requires an organisation to adopt the right toolset, culture, and processes. Implementing a Capability Model of DevOps starts with creating a roadmap and conducting a technology readiness analysis to understand the organisation's current state. TRA will help you determine the gaps and prioritise the recommended actions. - Next, we recommend that you conduct a Capability Quick Scan and a Technology Readiness Analysis to understand the gaps and recommended actions. - Finally, we recommend that you put the recommended actions in place and measure the impact. The Capability Model of DevOps will help organisations to identify and prioritise the areas for improvement and determine which process changes are required to adopt DevOps successfully. A Capability Model of DevOps requires an organisation to adopt the right toolset, culture, and processes. Into which processes are most likely to be associated with the areas of improvement identified in the Capability Quick Scan.

Capability and Process Analytics: A Tool for Understanding Management of DevOps and Processes. This tool will help you determine whether an organisation is using a process. The tool will also help you understand how many processes are in use. This information can be helpful for planning, identifying processes and managing process timeframes. The data collected will also provide insight into which processes are most likely to be associated with the areas of improvement identified in the Capability Quick Scan.

The Capability Quick Scan provides a quick, easy-to-use way to evaluate an organisation's readiness to adopt DevOps practices. Once you have done the Capability assessment, is it enough for DevOps embracement? Too early to say. But this will give a quick look at the capabilities and its gap. It will help you to address this effectively.

Some DevOps Coaches conduct the capability mappings and scanning through structured interviews, Questionnaires and face-to-face to determine the capabilities.

CHAPTER 11: PERFORM BUY OR REUSE ANALYSIS

Buy or Reuse analysis: Based on established criteria, the process of determining whether a product should be developed, purchased, or reused.

When it comes to DevOps transformation and software development, there is much noise out there. Everyone is saying something different or has opinions on what will work best for you as an organisation. That's because we are in the early stages of these movements, and every company faces unique challenges. During this time, the organisation's Steering committee or Devops Steering committee members tend to save costs. Hence, they easily choose to reuse the current software in their landscape, including obsolete versioned software that approaches the end of life. However, this will possess and carry the risk as the easy choice was not the right choice!

This chapter isn't going to give you more noise but clarity. It will provide insight into the pros and cons of using your software versus buying it from a vendor. Along with a few other things that will help make your decision easier. One of the biggest hurdles many organisations face when moving from the waterfall software development approach to Agile/DevOps is knowing which path is right for them. This chapter will address the challenges and provide the steps for performing a build or reuse analysis for software automation and tool selection strategies.

Define Your Goals and Objectives

Before reviewing any tools or processes, you must define your goals and objectives to make an informed selection. You may be targeting to improve a specific process, replace an existing tool, or consider a hybrid approach to automate multiple flows. Be sure to consider the following factors when defining your goals and objectives. First, why does the process exist in the first place? - Understanding the reason for the existing process will help you identify the key metrics that indicate a need for improvement. For example, suppose the current process is manually intensive. In that case, the critical metric may be the time it takes to complete the process. Are there any areas of low or weak performance? - Poor performance metrics can often indicate areas that can improve. For example, suppose you have a manual code review process that takes more than ten days. In that case, it may be a good indicator that you need to improve that process by implementing new software that can perform code reviews. e.g., /- SonarQube, Codacy.

Assess the Current State of Affairs

The next step is to assess the current situation, which includes reviewing the existing processes and any current tools. It will also be helpful to have any processes that may not be currently automated but that you want to automate or partially automate. This information will help you to identify where there may be opportunities for improvement and provide you with context to assess your selection criteria. First, review the current processes - Note any areas that could be automated or improved. Next, look at the existing tools - Be sure to check the usage of the software and how they have been implemented. Finally, identify missing processes - Look for any currently manual processes that you want to automate or partially automate.

Select a Tool or Process to Review

Based on your goals and objectives and the current state of affairs, select one or more tools or processes to review, such as Continuous Integration, Continuous Deployment, Automated Code Review, Code Analysis, Code Coverage, and other processes and tools. Select tools or processes based on factors such as the following.

Check Out the Tool or Process and Determine the Effort

After selecting the tool or process to review:

1. Check it out, and observe the current process.
2. Include stakeholders in this process to ensure you understand how the tool is used or how the process works.
3. After reviewing the tool or process, determine the effort required to build or implement the tool or process.

Estimate the cost of development and maintenance

After determining the cost of development, estimate the cost of maintenance. High maintenance indicates you may need to make lots of effort during the operational phase. Hence it would be better to buy as the support will be taken care of by Vendor. Moreover, while spending support costs, you will be secured by SLAs.

Identify Critical Functions to be Automated

After determining the effort to implement the selected tool or process, it is time to identify the essential functions that need to be automated. When recalling these critical functions, be sure to consider the following factors.

Estimate the Effort

After identifying the essential functions to be automated, it is time to estimate the effort required to automate those functions. When evaluating the effort for these functions, consider the following factors.

Perform a build or reuse analysis

After estimating the cost of development and maintenance for the tool or process and identifying the essential functions to be automated, it is time to perform a build or reuse analysis. To help you determine if it is better to build the functionality from scratch or reuse an existing software or process. When performing a build or reuse analysis, consider the following factors.

Need Proof of Concept

Before buying any software, a good idea is to perform a proof of concept. The best way to decide which software to buy is to see what it does and how it does it. You can then decide if the software is a good fit for your organisation. For example, if you have been working with a vendor and have picked the software you want, you can do a proof of concept at that time. That way, you know you are buying the right software for your organisation. To build your software, you can also do a proof of concept. In this case, you want to ensure you are making the right software to meet your organisation's needs.

Calculate ROI and TCO

Calculating the ROI and TCO can determine if it is better to build or reuse by comparing the relative values. Including the TCO in an enterprise software ROI calculation is essential, but it's frequently overlooked or underestimated. Let us See what to include in the TCO estimate and use it to make better software purchasing decisions by considering the ROI.

The Total Cost of Ownership (TCO) for enterprise software includes all direct and indirect expenses. Therefore, it is a crucial part of the ROI calculation. This Segment of this chapter looks at the lifetime expenses associated with enterprise software, which include three categories:

1. Off-the-shelf
2. cloud-based
3. custom software is just a few hybrid options available.

We will not go into detail about these options, but they will incur many of the expenses described below. This Segment aims to explain the estimate of the costs associated with developing software so that TCO and ROI estimates are more realistic and meaningful.

Startup Cost, a.k.a CAPEX: Usually, Organisations need to remember the startup costs. This Startup cost will occur when you introduce the new software into your ecosystems. So let's see what expenses have been a portion of this cost type.

Off-the-shelf software usually has an up-front software cost and user licenses. Be sure to include any finance charges and provisioning for size up.

Hardware cost comprises Server and storage costs. However, cloud software does not include the software's price and other factors like backup and disaster recovery.

Implementation is setting up, configuring, and testing software to use in production. Custom software is typically configured as part of the development process, but all software has this requirement. In addition to setting up backups, disaster recovery, and other things, this category includes the costs of setting up and configuring software.

In some scenarios, it may not be economical to migrate data from the old to the new system so that the old system can archive in a read-only mode.

There are two user licenses for off-the-shelf software: named users and Parallel users. For the cloud, licenses are usually named. This does not apply to custom software.

Training is one of the most significant expenses when implementing new software. It applies to all software types and includes training end users, helpdesk, and system administration employees.

Enterprises no longer function independently; instead, they must interface with other company systems. Using the plain version of off-the-shelf software is usually preferable rather than customising it to fit your needs. However, it can make future updates impossible or difficult. Custom code no longer functions due to an update frequently preventing future updates.

Operating expenses a.k.a OPEX:

Clearly, everyone can say that the production phases involve certain expenses.

It's common for off-the-shelf software to be sold on yearly contracts, including maintenance and support. On the other hand, with custom software, support and ongoing costs are often higher than the initial development costs over the product's lifetime. Usually, this doesn't apply to cloud software.

Patches are the cost of applying security and bug-fix patches to off-the-shelf software is what applies here.

If the number of employees increases with off-the-shelf software, more user licenses must be purchased. If the number of employees decreases, there are no refunds. Cloud applications, in most cases, are priced monthly, but they usually require an annual contract. Therefore, the cost of employee usage rises as the number of employees increases. If the number of employees decreases, the price may fall. However, a price fall usually applies when the contract renewal takes place.

Companies need to train their employees to handle new personnel. In addition, cloud vendors may require some training as they push new enhancements.

Custom software, where the company must pay developers to provide new functionality as needed, e.g., when the business environment changes or new regulations come into effect. And any benefit from enhancements. For example, project or product management and documentation costs must also be included.

Help desk and system administrator support also need to be included in this expense, as well as a few analysts/developers supporting the system. Remember that you must use the fully burdened employee cost and include the costs of managing them.

Backup and hot failover are among the many disaster recoveries and high availability options. Unfortunately, Off-the-shelf, and custom software are very costly to hot failover. Cloud solutions are often included as part of the standard package, except for smaller firms. However, cloud services come at an extra cost in addition to being able to recover if the cloud provider shuts down.

It's essential to account for indirect costs when calculating what it costs to run software in a data centre, such as security, data centre maintenance, and data centre management. A data centre is where computer hardware is housed and maintained. The hardware is running with off-the-shelf and custom software. A hosted data centre refers to the monthly cost of running the hardware.

An inordinate amount of downtime can negatively impact a business, particularly when it comes to custom software. Since custom programmes aren't as extensively tested as cloud or off-the-shelf programmes, downtime expenses may be higher. In addition, cloud providers invest in things like hot failover to keep their customers satisfied, which may make their software more vulnerable to failure.

It's a systematic method of allocating a physical asset's cost over its useful life. Because cloud software is usually an operational expense, depreciation does not apply to it.

Upgrades are available for off-the-shelf software throughout its lifespan. However, these updates can be massive, costly, time-consuming, and risky for the corporation. Custom software updates also need to include when a new version is launching. Cloud software does not have updates because most vendors continually upgrade their software.

The cost of securing an application, mainly if it is accessible outside the firewall, is a matter of security. The cloud provider pays for Cloud software, which is not included in this category.

Since this is a non-technical Chapter, hence readers may feel distracted. Apologies! The underline point is that readers must analyse all the suggested topics discussed in this chapter. At the same time, assessing, buying, or reusing your software.

PART 4 – MOKITAS IN THE LEAN ROOM

CHAPTER 1: MODERNISE THE CHANGE MANAGEMENT

Change Management An adaptive strategy that balances exploration and action.

DevOps culture has taken the software development world by storm. More and more companies are implementing DevOps principles in their software development processes, enabling them to create better products faster. With a focus on team collaboration, accelerated release cycles, and data-driven decision-making, DevOps is changing how software is produced and deployed. And while many organisations have started adopting these practices, only some have implemented them successfully. However, that's not to say it's an impossible feat. The success of your implementation of DevOps largely depends on how you set up your process from the get-go. Implementing change management can go a long way in streamlining your new strategies and creating a stable workflow for all team members.

In this chapter, let's see how to modernise your Change management and the key steps to achieve this. The easiest way of modernising your change is the Lean method. Yes! It is just a clue. Let's look at the aspects of the clue.

What is Lean Change Management?

Lean change management is a strategy for implementing change more effectively. The goal of lean change management is to make changes that are sustainable, predictable, and easy to implement across the organisation. Lean change management focuses on how to create change that is more effective and less wasteful. In addition, lean change management focuses on how projects are being implemented. Organisations can then find ways to make their change more effective, less wasteful, and easier to implement.

Some of us need clarification about lean change and process management. So let's clear that first.

The critical distinction between lean change management and lean process improvement is that lean process improvement focuses on changing processes without affecting human efficiency. In contrast, human efficiency can only be improved by increasing human productivity. On the other hand, lean process improvement focuses on changing processes without affecting human efficiency. Let us flip thru now.

What is Lean Process Improvement?

Lean process improvement is a method of reducing the impact of change on the efficiency and productivity of an organisation. Primarily due to the close relationship between human productivity and efficiency.

Lean process improvement focuses on changing how an organisation functions, ensuring that it is highly efficient and effective. Due to the facts of organisation's efficiency and effectiveness are related. Therefore, lean process improvement is about studying how something functions.

Lean processes have been implemented for at least one year of continuous improvement. Still, they don't significantly impact operational or operational efficiency or effectiveness due to being implemented Incrementally.

Why is Lean Change Management Important in a DevOps Environment?

When implementing new change in an organisation, there's always the risk of creating more harm than good. Exceptionally accurate in the world of DevOps, where the focus is on speed and agility. Change is carefully analysed and implemented in a controlled fashion in a traditional software development environment. This behaviour leads to a slow bureaucratic process with little room for mistakes. And when it comes to DevOps, implementing change is even more crucial. After all, DevOps is all about change. Its focus is on creating a more streamlined product development and deployment process. However, change is often not managed effectively in this environment. Instead of creating structured change, squads are left to their gizmos and to make their processes as they go along. This siloed approach can lead to an inconsistent and inefficient workflow. Bottom line? You must implement it leanly to implement change in a DevOps environment.

Make the Road to DevOps Implementation Easier

As we have already noted, implementing change can take time and effort. In a DevOps environment, where change is the name of the game, it is even more difficult. So, to ease the path to DevOps implementation, it's essential to establish a change management plan from the start. Developing a strategy for how you will roll out your DevOps changes, which you will involve, and how much change to expect. First, determine what type of change you want to implement. There are several types of changes that organisations can implement. The most common is a change in the way the company operates. Other types of change include changing the organisation's strategy, structure, or culture. You also need to identify the stakeholders who will involve in the change. Change cannot implement effectively in a vacuum, so whom will you apply in your process?

Determine Culture Change Needed for Success

Before implementing your change, you need to know whether your organisation can handle it. Here is where culture change comes into play. Companies with a creative or innovative process are often resistant to change because they have a Proven-process in place. And they want to make sure it is clear from unnecessary change. And while this is fine in the proper context, it can be detrimental in a DevOps environment. After all, the very premise of DevOps is that things need to change. It's about creating a more streamlined process for creating and deploying products. So how do you know if your company can handle the change? The best way is to survey the team and ask them what they think about the proposed changes. It's essential to gauge how the team feels about the proposed changes and determine what factors contribute to their feelings.

Setting Proper Expectations

After you've determined that your organisation can handle the change and that the team is ready for it, you need to set proper expectations. With every change, there will be winners and losers. Identify the people early thru Some lean Change techniques and tools. We will read through our next chapter on how essential it is to let them know how they will be affected. By This way, they can accept their fate and move on. You can do this by hosting a change management meeting with key stakeholders and team members. You can discuss the proposed changes at this meeting and explain how they will affect the organisation. You can also use a change management tool to track expectations. Many change management tools exist, but a CMDB solution is the best. A CMDB solution provides change management features to help you track the progress and impact of your changes.

Create a Roadmap of Support Tools

After you've implemented your changes and your team is running the show, you need to look ahead and see what you can do to support them. Here is where creating a roadmap of support tools is essential. A roadmap of support tools is simply a list of support tools you will implement to help your team run more effectively.

Several tools can help your team run more effectively, including:

Change management software: A change management application can help you track, manage, and report your changes.

Issue tracking software: Issue tracking software is a valuable tool for teams working in DevOps. It is designed to keep track of all the broken things in need of repair.

Release management software: Release management software is designed to help you keep track of your product release cycles.

Service desk software: Service desk software is designed to provide IT support to your organisation's end users.

CMDB software: A CMDB application can help you track your team's progress and manage their impact on the organisation.

Plan for new roles and responsibilities

After implementing your changes, new roles and responsibilities will pop up in your organisation. Thinking about how you will support these new roles and responsibilities is essential. You can create a change management plan and identify the tools your team needs to succeed. For example, suppose your team is responsible for creating release notes after a product release. It would be best if you implemented a change to integrate this process into your release management software.

Plan for Infrastructure Changes

Whenever you implement a change, there's a chance that it will break something. To minimise such risk, build a release plan that includes changes to your infrastructure. It's much essential when you're implementing DevOps changes that have the potential to harm your infrastructure. After all, you can only implement changes to the software once you know how they will impact the infrastructure. Therefore, after you've implemented your changes, you need to assess their impact on the infrastructure. You can create a release report detailing all the changes you've executed and their effect on the infrastructure.

In a Nutshell, Change is inevitable and desirable. However, it keeps organisations fresh and innovative only if the change is implemented effectively. So it's essential to manage change in a structured way to ensure it achieves the desired results. If you want your company to succeed in the DevOps world, you need to implement change in a lean manner. Lean change management is about creating effective and less wasteful change. That's why it's important to implement change in a structured way:

1. You need to identify what kind of change you want to implement.
2. Involve your stakeholders, and determine whether your organisation can handle it.
3. Set proper expectations, create a roadmap of support tools, and plan for infrastructure changes.

CHAPTER 2: BLAST RADIUS DIAGRAM

Blast radius: Mapping out the intended and possible unintended consequences will assist you in understanding.

Change has unintended consequences. No matter how much or how often you socialise your changes, predicting how people will react to a change is still challenging until they hear it.

When it comes To DevOps Transformation, most organisations need to remember that they are trying to achieve a single piece of flow. Hence, later stage of the Transformation, the price of miscalculating the changes is lofty.

When talking about Change management, the change management process is only complete with a blast radius diagram. First, managers must understand the impact of their decisions on different parts of an organisation. The advantage of the Blast Radius diagram is that it helps managers determine the most vulnerable or fragile areas in possible change, which can then be addressed before making any significant changes to lessen any negative impacts.

The blast radius diagram is the tool used to measure the impact of change on an organisation. This diagram aims to calculate the changes in the behaviour and structure of an organisation caused by implementing a particular change.

Let's look at a blast radius diagram.

It can also analyse how different sections of an organisation will respond to a change and how it will affect the entire company. The objective of this tool is to include everything that needs consideration when contemplating a specific shift.

For example, an organisation must understand that a Blast Radius Diagram is a convenient tool for mapping the impact of change on the entire project. Additionally, it gives an overview of all risks that might happen.

With a Blast radius diagram, it is possible to map out all the possible changes that may happen to the project and their respective impacts. Ignoring the blast radius exercise can create some risks for the project's stakeholders, so it is essential to be mindful of any changes before they happen to avoid any negative consequences.

Asides from Change Management, this is an excellent tool for risk assessment that helps determine how much changes will affect dependent projects or tasks or what other potential consequences of this change.

It also helps prioritise risky changes and identify the risk to each shift. So now it's time to look around the process of creating a Blast radius diagram.

Identify fundamental change(s): The stage in which DevOps coaches and change initiators work with a designated change manager to identify the actual change(s) at the centre of the boom radius of change. It would be helpful to list the fundamental process changes at the heart of what needs to be changed.

Identify Directly Impacted Stakeholders: These are stakeholder groups that are doing the work being affected.

Identify Indirectly Impacted affected parties: Complete each component of the indirectly impacted region, including "Indirectly Impacted affected parties:"

Internal or external parties who contribute ideas or information necessary to finish the influenced work

Customers are those internal or external stakeholders who depend on the impacted work's outputs to finish their work.

Approvers: Internal or external stakeholders who examine, accept, or provide the go-ahead for the affected job.

Spotting the Interesting Parties: Determine the parties who will impact the change and who will be critical to the organisation's or their teams' overall performance. Although these Parties do not fall under those directly or indirectly touched categories, they need to be kept in the loop.

1. Directly impacted Interested Change Parties - the people going through the change in play will be directly involved or affected by it.
2. Indirectly impacted Change Parties - the people who may not be going through the change but are still significantly affected by it and should have input on how to adjust to accommodate these changes.

These change parties may be members of different teams that carry out various tasks, but they all rely on a common goal to proceed.

Monitors - individuals who can review

Impact Assessment: Assess the level of change impact for each stakeholder group as High, Medium, or Low, and label accordingly.

- **High:** The implementation of the changes will significantly impact stakeholders.
- **Medium:** Some effects will feel by These parties, but the implementation of the changes is not significant
- **Low:** The implementation of the changes will not significantly affect stakeholders.

Assess Level of Support: Label each stakeholder group as either:

It is essential to categorise stakeholders into three groups to understand the level of support. The first group consists of early adopters willing to try out new technologies and experiment with them. The second group consists of fence-sitters who are undecided about whether they want to adopt the technology. Finally, the third group comprises immovables, those who already have a system that cannot be updated and whose livelihood is tied to the old system.

Well, you now have a fundamental understanding of Blast radius. What's next? Let me state the 5 Tips for Creating a Blast Radius Diagram in Change Management.

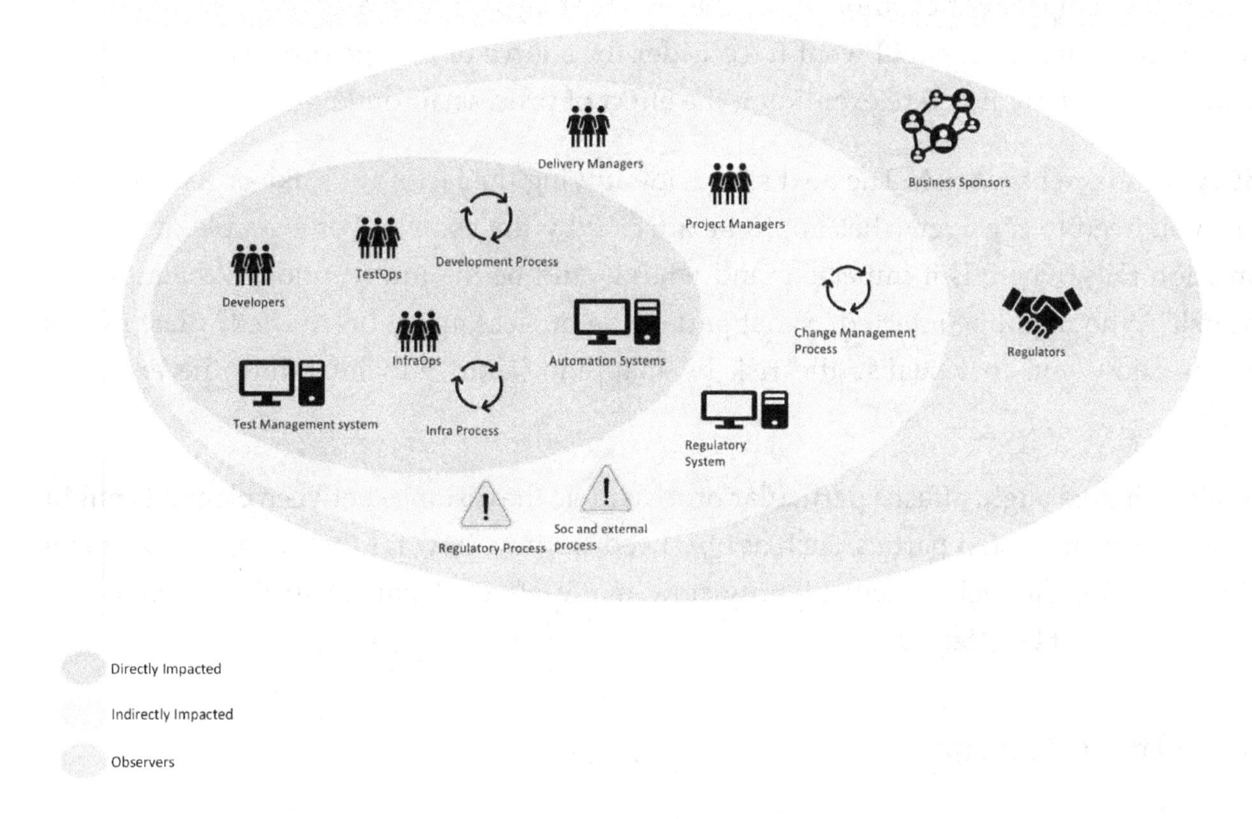

As you can see from the diagram above, a blast radius is the distance from the point of origin where things are affected. In other words, a blast radius is an area that experiences the effects of Changes. If DevOps Change goes off in an organisation, for example, where does it apply? How many Impacts does it make? How many Change parties are affected? These are all questions that a blast radius diagram answers. It's an easy way to visualise and analyse how things will impact by an event or change. Let's look at five ways you can create your blast radius diagram:

Determine the point of origin: The first thing you need to do when creating a blast radius diagram determines the origin point. Everything hangs on this first and most fundamental fact, no matter how complex the chart may get. You'll also want to consider how the event or change might happen. For example, suppose you're analysing how a Change might affect a process area. In that case, you'll want to consider the source of change (process automation, for example) similarly if you're examining the effect of process automation.

Identify the elements at risk: The next step is identifying the factors at stake or risk. In other words, you need to consider what might be affected by the change. For example, if process automation fails, where is it impacted, and what would be the interruption? Which parties are at risk? Who might be infected? What part of the process might be affected? Blast radius diagrams allow you to visualise the risk by mapping it out and including the expected distance.

So, while a change might affect a particular process area, the distance between elements might vary. Similarly, interested parties, such as QA, need to know how far this change impact will continue. Again, this helps them identify how many affected parties in the surrounding process area might be affected.

Define their distance from the origin point:

Now that you've identified the elements at risk and their distance from the origin point, you can draw lines between them to show how far each element is from the others. For example, if you're creating a diagram to show how a change affects a process area, you could create a line between each process area, such as Development and QA, that shows how far they are from the source of the change. When you make a blast radius diagram, it's essential to include the expected distance. This helps you visualise how far each element is from the origin point. It also lets you think about how far each segment is from the other.

Find their distance from each other: The next step is to find the distance between each element on the diagram. You can draw a line from one aspect to the other and measure the distance between them. For example, if you're analysing CI/CD Pipeline change, you can put each element on the diagram. You can then draw a line from each component to each process area to determine the distance between each by analysing the effects of CI/CD automation. You can then draw a line between each segment to determine their length from each other. Blast radius diagrams allow you to visualise these distances by mapping them out and including the expected space.

Draw your diagram: Once all the elements are mapped, you can start drawing the diagram. Blast radius diagrams are essential maps with circles and lines. The circles represent each element at risk, and the lines represent their distance from each other. Blast radius diagrams allow you to visualise the risk by mapping it out and including the expected space. They're a great way to imagine how an event or accident will affect a specific area. They help you think about how far each element is from the origin point and how far each element is from the other.

In a nutshell, Blast radius diagrams are an easy way to visualise how an event or accident might affect a particular area. They allow you to map out the risks by putting each element at risk on the diagram and including their distance from one another. They're a great way to get a big-picture view of how things will be affected and help you think about the best course of action moving forward.

CHAPTER 3: HANDY BECKHARD AND HARRIS CHANGE PROCESS

Beckhard-Harris Change Equation: A basic tool for forecasting workplace changes. It takes into account today's shifting landscape and can help you decide whether your modifications will be successful.

When it comes to DevOps transformation, more than the Blast radius is needed. There are a few other process combinations that will help ease your adoption. One is Beckhard and Harris change.

What is Beckhard and Harris Change Process?

The Beckhard and Harris Change Process is a five-step technique that supports organisations in recognising the need for transformation and putting forward the necessary initiatives to make that change happen. An internal organisation study, evaluating whether change is needed, carrying out a gap analysis, action planning, and successfully managing the transition are the five procedures that make up these five steps. The goal of this technique is to provide an outline of the steps that need to follow to execute change properly.

Stages of Beckhard and Harris Change Process?

The Beckhard and Harris Change Process consist of five distinct stages.

Internal Organisational Analysis: The first step towards implementing change in your organisation is to figure out people's feelings on change. If you want to ask them questions about the reform, make sure you speak to various employees to get a sense of their opinions. To provide more clarity, the individuals responsible for change must identify which hirelings will most likely resist change. In addition, individuals who are leading the change are the ones who are responsible for determining any external forces that can make the shift take longer.

Identify the Change needs: To generate the necessary motivation, you must identify the necessity of making a change. All primary change agents must agree that the change is needed for the organisation's growth and success. To achieve this, change agents need to be able to define the path they want the organisation to take, why implementing the change will assist in moving the organisation closer to its desired state, and what disadvantages arise from not implementing it.

Carrying the Gap Analysis: Before any change can be implemented, the first thing that needs to happen is a study of the existing gaps. Before we can achieve any changes, agents of change must evaluate the gaps between the current state of the organisation and the state that is wanted for the organisation. It is of the utmost importance to articulate a vision for the organisation's future, which necessitates identifying deviations from that vision.

Action Planning Stage: Placing the action plan for the change into action happens at the process's action planning stage. Those driving the changes must identify the Key actors in the process so that they may be more explicit. (i.e., who will be responsible for executing the adjustments and who will be most impacted by the changes). The personnel responsible for implementing the change have been provided with an outline of the responsibilities incumbent upon them to carry out.

Managing Transition: Taking Charge of the Situation After the change has been implemented, those responsible for implementing it now have the added responsibility of regularly evaluating the change's progression and modifying it as they see fit.

Beckhard and Harris Change Formula

There's a formula for predicting when an organisation or individual will change, and it's called the Beckhard and Harris Change formula. The following conditions need to be met for an organisation or individual to change:

The change formula is

D*V*F>R

D = DISSATISFACTION

V = VISION FOR CHANGE

F = FIRST STEPS

R = RESISTANCE TO CHANGE

This change formula also says that for change to happen, all three parts on the left side, Desire, Vision, and First Steps, must be present. Therefore, there is always some Resistance to change. So, if any element of the equation is missing, the product equals zero, which is smaller than the original number.

Dissatisfaction: Every change begins with two aspects. Everyone wants to be happy. But often, a person's current reality is mired in pain without a clear path to change. The second is a willingness to seek alternatives. Change is possible. But leaders should never make assumptions about others, understanding the same need for change as they do themselves.

Vision for Change: When people want change but can't see a "way forward," they may experience rage, depression, frustration, anxiety, or apathy. Rarely positive. Vision mobilises change-driven energy. A shared vision answers, "What do we want to develop or accomplish?" It doesn't matter where the vision originated in the organisation, but it must be articulate so that individuals are encouraged — not required — to share it.

First Steps: Without action, vision is meaningless because it's just a "building in the cloud". You'll need a plan on how to execute your ideas. Employees will often become disappointed if an organisation has a clear vision for the change to implement. They might feel like their work is pointless and that any effort they put in won't lead to anything significant. The effects of this can also link to feelings of irritation and powerlessness. Which often leads to apathy and cynicism.

To successfully involve members of an organisation in the process of change, you need to provide them with the opportunity to describe their reality. The purpose of the forums is to consult on the future and devise action plans for realising this vision.

When exploring the process of implementing organisational change and the affected stakeholders, consider the stages of Dissatisfaction, Vision, and First Steps.

- At the level of the whole change initiative,
- The individual impact of the change

Resistance to change: Creating the product of Desire, Vision, and First Steps is greater than Resistance to Change. It is essential to figure out how much resistance there is. Organisations don't resist change: people do. Even though some people don't accept change for personal reasons, some general principles exist. First, people usually resist change when they

Anticipate that employees will lose something important in the change and in some cased lack of trust in those promoting or driving the change. When it comes to huge change transformation, many employees think they will negatively impact the company if they don't have enough understanding about the proposed changes

Some believe they will need help to keep up with changing technology and need help with their job. In contrast, some assume the change is outside the organisation's best interests.

In a Nutshell, the most effective way of dealing with resistance is to involve the stakeholders in shaping the elements on the left side of the change equation. And hence to examine the "need for change", creating a Vision of a preferred future, and determining the First Steps toward achieving the vision, the system not only becomes richer in wisdom and passion but will address any actual or potential concerns about an upcoming change.

CHAPTER 4: CHANGE VOLUME ASSESSMENT PRACTISES

Change volume assessment: To assess the effectiveness of a particular change management initiative.

Change management is usually a more complex and time-consuming process. It takes work to manage these changes in a way that recognises some areas of the business. However, it ensures frequent checks and balances to ensure you're on the dot with user impact, company policies, regulatory compliance, and data security. Managing change within an enterprise can be a complex task. First, change management should determine how changes will work, what techniques must be utilised, and which methods are best applied. There are many solutions to change management and various ways to plan how you manage it. In addition, there is a range of different approaches you can use that continue to work in any situation.

DevOps and Change Management

More and more organisations are turning to DevOps as it speeds up development cycles and helps customers see improvements in their products. However, changes usually happen serially or reactively, and DevOps can be rugged in large enterprises. So it's essential to consider these factors.

Change management frameworks help with company-wide changes that may involve dependencies or other risks. DevOps is a more Agile approach to IT Management that focuses on streams of small and frequent changes that can implement as they're completed. It's perfect for environments undergoing smaller, continuous updates.

DevOps is an application of automation that fits nicely with a change management process. While these seem to be competing for resources, DevOps will improve code quality and speed software delivery, which should improve your business.

To succeed with DevOps, you need to clearly define and communicate the changes in a way that doesn't interrupt workflows. This must be challenging because DevOps is about more than just improving the software. It's about changing an organisation's culture and how people work together.

Change must track throughout the development lifecycle, shared with other systems and personnel, and understood concerning other intersection points. Here is where the DevOps approach comes in. Enterprises can gradually achieve higher quality levels by refining processes and integrating business systems and tools. Suppose an organisation is starting on the DevOps journey. In that case, there is often a need for more communication between departments regarding software development. However, you can break down this barrier with DevOps.

When introducing DevOps into an enterprise, it's crucial to meet these criteria:

- You have probably already heard things like 'fail early and fix early, 'iterations', and 'sprint planning. With these agile concepts, time flies - who wouldn't want to succeed at work?
- A company's culture is meant to encourage collaboration and discourage disruptive information.
- There is a passion for implementing organisational changes that result in a more sustainable time-to-market.

Changes in Policies.

When introducing new changes in a company, it is often best to update your security policies. Revising security policies will ensure you start on the right foot and keep your company safe from risks. In addition, a secure software development process is often a good idea early on. Security is essential to every company's success. Make sure you test the product early on and add checkpoints that promote a sense of security with Security scans, penetration tests and security measures.

By eliminating policies that keep development and IT operations separate. You can collaborate with DevOps teams earlier in the design process, which can help anticipate infrastructural changes and minimise disruption. You can also use the tool in production environments to improve workflow and reduce documentation.

Create Process and procedure baselines.

It's always good to refer to the process inventory and prepare the baseline checklist and its procedures, workflows, and appropriate approvals. Before introducing automation around the existing processes. Few processes listed out here

- Development and Engineering practice processes.
- Procedures for high-level organisational changes
- Security and compliance procedures
- Change and Quality assurance procedures
- Project and Business process procedure

These processes and procedure reviews will help to create a few discoveries on DevOps processes such as CI/CD and Deployment, Rollback environment provisioning automation.

Once all the above prerequisites are done, you can start with the Change volume assessment.

What is Change Volume Assessment?

No one-size-fits-all strategy for change management makes it challenging to develop a plan. However, various strategies may be worth considering to increase the likelihood of success.

A Change Volume Assessment helps ensure you have a detailed plan for moving forward. It provides a way to assess what is involved in change and allows you to take measures to ensure success. When modernising this process, you'll need to identify it at the start of the project.

- What parts of your business will be affected?
- Who is impacted?
- What resources could be influenced or require some investment?

The process of carrying out a Change volume assessment centres on figuring out the stages of the change effort. The idea is to figure out where you are in the stages and then target your communication strategy accordingly. Gathered through individual conversations, surveys, and raw data analysis of business operations, this information helps to guide successful change management planning moving forward.

To succeed in a change process, you need to identify the outcomes you want to achieve and the impacts of this change. Perform an impact analysis of your organisation's readiness for these changes before proceeding, and finally rescoped the change management initiative parameters based on expectations and commitments across the business

In a Nutshell, many businesses try to make changes without first considering the ramifications, which can lead to severe issues. When contemplating a change for your organisation, assessing the costs and advantages is critical before proceeding. Change Volume Assessment is a tool for determining an organisation's level of support. Aside from that, it can aid in analysing future changes and their influence on an organisation.

CHAPTER 5: MINIMISING WORK IN PROGRESS AND MAKING WORK VISIBLE

Reduce Work in Progress: Work reduction process utilising real-time production monitoring and digital work instructions to optimise bandwidth and quality.

DevOps transformation is a continuing challenge in almost every organisation. When you work towards DevOps transformation, your work in progress (WIP) will increase, and so will the hand-off complexity. However, there are many ways through which you can minimise WIP to reduce hand-off complexity, make work visible, reducing wait times and hand-off complexity in your transformation journey.

Let's look at some tried-and-true strategies for minimising work in progress (WIP) and making it simpler to see what must be done next. These strategies include lowering wait times, lowering hand-off complexity, and reducing hand-off complexity in DevOps Transformation efforts. Some organisations need to catch up on these in the earlier stage of their DevOps Conception if these critical steps still need to be considered.

Establish a constant improvement mindset

DevOps Transformation is a never-ending journey. There will always be new technology to learn, new processes to implement, and new ways to collaborate. Constant improvement is the key to success in this journey. Presidents and CEOs are always looking for ways to improve their organisations. In their search, they often find that their employees are more interested in defending their turf than finding ways to improve and innovate. It would help if the team clarified that any improvement is welcome. The team must be the ones who ask for ideas on how to improve. They will find that people take great pride in doing their jobs better and helping the company move forward. Once they have an improvement mindset, it's easy to make these proven suggestions happen.

Avoid hand-offs and make everything visible to everyone.

In many transformation efforts, you'll find people doing many hand-offs. They'll be handing off requirements to engineers, engineers to testers and testers to operations. You'll end up with hand-offs from one engineering team to another, from one product team to another, from one services team to another, from marketing to sales and from sales to operations. You'll also find hand-offs from customers to product management, from product management to engineering and from sales to product management. Once you see hand-offs, you can reduce them and try to make everything visible to everyone. You may not need certain hand-offs. You can reduce the frequency of others. If you do need hand-offs, you can try to make them visible. If a hand-off needs to happen, you can write it on a board and have it visible to everyone who needs to see it. That way, everyone who needs to know will see it.

Use short development cycles (iterations or sprints)

If you're using Agile or Scrum, you'll probably have one to two weeks of development cycles. With this cycle, you can reduce hand-offs to a large degree. For example, you can have one team working on their assignment, and when they have done the job, they'll hand it off to the next team. When you use short development cycles, you can also make work visible to everyone. As your team is working on an assignment, you can put it on the board and keep it visible to the rest of the organisation. Your team might need to use a Kanban board to make work visible. If so, keep work visualise in the columns representing different stages of transformation.

Rotate your engineers to different Tribes

Suppose you have different Tribes in your organisation. In that case, you can minimise hand-offs by rotating your engineers through the other Tribes. For example, let's say you have a Tribe that is responsible for Sales Transformation, a Tribe that is responsible for Marketing Transformation and a Tribe that is responsible for Operations Transformation. You can assign your engineers to these Tribes. This way, they're working with people in the same profession. This will help them learn more and make work more visible. If your engineers are contributing to different Tribes, you can put the assignments on the board. This will help make work visible to everyone who needs to know. They can remove it from the board when they finish a specific task. This will allow people to see what has been done and what needs to do next.

Don't build too many things at once (known as WIP Limits)

If your organisation has an extended WIP Limit, you'll end up with too many things in progress. With too many items in hand-off, you'll increase complexity and make work slower. To tackle the WIP Limit, you can follow the theory of constraints. You can use the theory of constraints to identify the constraint in your hand-off process. If you decide to specify the theory of constraints, you should hire an external consultant. It would be best if you did not use a consultant to do the work. Instead, you should hire a consultant to help you make the right decision. When you identify the constraint, you can reduce it by maximising the other activities. You can do this by making work visible, reducing the hand-off complexity and wait times.

Use automation to make humans more effective rather than replacing them.

When you automate something, you use technology to make humans more effective. When you use automation, you're not trying to replace your people. Instead, you're trying to make them more effective. You can use automation to help reduce hand-off complexity and make work visible. You can use automation to make it easier to see what needs to do next. Communicate with your team members as you add automation to your transformation efforts. Let them know what changes are happening and how automation will make their jobs easier. When you implement automation, it's a good idea to keep it visible. Put the automation on a Kanban board and make the automation visible to everyone who needs to know.

Create a simple, clear, and precise Definition of Done (DoD) for each hand-off step

As you transform your organisation and hand-offs, you might encounter a few hand-off steps where the definition of done (DoD) needs to be clarified. That's why you should create a simple, clear, and precise description of done for every hand-off step. Then, if you need to implement hand-offs or dependencies, you can use a Kanban board to keep track of them. That way, you'll make all dependencies visible to everyone. That will help you avoid hand-offs that need to be clarified and precise.

Make dependencies visible through task tagging.

When you work towards digital transformation, you'll have many different dependencies. You'll need to wait for one team to finish working on something before you can start working on another thing. When you have dependencies, they make hand-offs more complex, increase wait times and make it more difficult to see what needs to be done next. When you have tasks with dependencies, you can make them visible by tagging the task with the person working on it. If a task has no dependencies, you can tag it with people who should be aware of it. When you tag tasks with people, ensure you add only a little information. Just set the person's name and the task they're working on. You don't need to place an explanation.

Set a cadence for your release process

You'll need to release new features and upgrades when transforming your organisation towards DevOps. To do that, you might have a periodical release such as weekly, biweekly, or Monthly. You might not see any dependencies when you have a continuous delivery process. However, you need a continuous delivery process. In that case, you'll need to wait for other people to finish working on something before you can start working on something else. That's why you should set a cadence for your release process. That way, you'll know when to expect releases. When you have a cadence for your release process, you can make work visible using a Kanban board. Put a release card on the board when you start working on it. Once you are done, move the card to the done column.

In a Nutshell, reducing the amount of work in progress (WIP) in your supply chain is crucial. Doing so will improve your value stream and overall organisation's efficiency. The best way to reduce WIP is to make work visible. Visibility into the work of the people and machines in your value stream will show you where there is excess WIP. You can use lean tools and techniques to reduce the WIP and make work visible. Another way to reduce WIP is to reduce hand-offs. When one person or team passes work off to another person or group, there is always a chance that they'll make a mistake. There is also a chance that the two parties need to communicate better, causing delays and WIP.

CHAPTER 6: MAKING CONTINUOUS IMPROVEMENT A DAILY HABIT WITH KATA MODEL

Kata: Consistent improvement requires structured practice.

In Japanese, the word "kata" implies "form" or "pair practice." It is a methodical approach to creating a culture of ongoing learning and development at all levels. A company's "motor memory" for continual learning is formed through its everyday routines and habits.

In martial arts, katas are physical drills that help practitioners understand the movements and stances necessary to perform complex techniques efficiently. These precise repetitions also allow students to feel how their muscles should react when executing specific strategies. This becomes muscle memory and forms the foundation for future learning in all situations.

Continuous improvement is a never-ending process. So, DevOps. Every DevOps initiative implementation leaves a footprint of Continuous Improvement. It requires an equally constant effort from all the members of your organisation. Suppose you want to improve a daily habit as part of your DevOps Metrics assessment. In that case, Kata Model can significantly help. It helps automate repetition, streamline processes, and identify core routines that must be strictly adhered to. This chapter will give critical insights into the advantages of using the Kata Model and its implementation steps. Let's get started!

What is Kata Model?

Kata is an Eastern philosophy where you learn and understand the "how" of a particular skill. Kata can then be applied to your real-world situations, thus leading to consistent and more effective outcomes. Kata Model is a model that outlines a step-by-step process that can use to set up daily improvement activities. With Kata, you can set up a system where everyone in the organisation follows a consistent approach to help the company achieve its goals. Kata is a systematic method of learning a particular skill, especially one that is highly specific and requires practice to achieve proficiency. It is an approach to teaching concepts and skills that involves making the methods and skills visible through a series of diagrams and implementing activities that are then repeated.

Why use Kata Model?

Every organisation should ask themselves the most crucial question: "why are we improving?" There is much talk about continuous business improvement, but only some organisations genuinely understand its importance. Can use improvement activities to set the foundation for future success. It can also help you better understand your strengths and weaknesses. Once you have this information, you can begin improving your processes. Improvement activities can help you identify bottlenecks in your process. Once you understand these problems, you can start to solve them. By identifying these issues, you can also find opportunities to reduce work time and improve efficiency.

Advantages of using the Kata Model

Helps in automating repetition: It helps in automating repetition. Identifying repetitive workflows and automating them is a core concept of Kata.

Streamlines processes: It helps streamline operations. In addition, it helps identify core routines that must be strictly adhered to.

Identifies and reduces bottlenecks in processes: It identifies and reduces bottlenecks in your process. It helps in identifying gaps and in closing them.

Gives focus to long-term goals: It helps provide focus to long-term goals. It also helps in aligning your team around the same goals.

Provides context for understanding your business: It provides context for understanding your business and what is happening in the industry. It helps you identify trends and explore the future of your business.

Steps to implement the Kata model in your organisation

There are seven steps to implement the Kata in your organisation. Let us apply these steps in your DevOps transformation as part of the Lean principle.

1. Identify the goals of your organisation (DevOps).
2. Identify the obstacles that are in your way to achieving these goals.
3. Identify your core routines.
4. Identify the activities that are contributing to your goals.
5. I Identify the workflow of the activities.
6. Identify the areas where you can automate the workflow.
7. Identify the people who can help you implement Kata.

Improvement Kata

Improvement Kata is the first Kata you will implement daily in your business. This Kata will focus on identifying your business's weaknesses and strengths. It will help you identify your business challenges and help find solutions for them. Strengths Weaknesses Opportunities How to use? Identify the weaknesses of your business. Weaknesses are areas where your business is facing challenges and problems. This is where the focus of the Kata should be. Next, identify the obstacles in your organisation.

Understand the Direction of the Target

As you implement the Kata, you will find yourself making incremental improvements. It is essential that you stay focused and don't get distracted. It is crucial that you identify these small but consistent improvements. As you improve your Kata, you will start noticing a change in your organisation. Your customers will experience reduced turnaround times. Your employees will feel more confident in their roles and responsibilities. And your stakeholders will receive better-quality results. Remember that these small improvements are needed to create a significant impact. It is essential to stay focused on your Kata and not get distracted by the daily hustle and bustle of working in the business.

Now Let's see how this can apply to DevOps transformation.

Having a common view of the direction in which you wish to move forward. It is effortless to get confused and adjust at random. That will only advance you in a clear direction if you have a theory of what you think is superior.

A clear and widespread awareness of the direction also gives people working on the improvement endeavour a sense of purpose. In contrast, it is much harder for people to become motivated when there is no apparent end.

It would be best if you built a Vision of DevOps transformation is done in an ideal condition to foster a sense of shared direction. Instead of focusing on outcomes, this vision should be process-oriented. The goal is to change the way work is done, not to start a DevOps transformation.

Suppose, if your organisation has a long-term vision for its DevOps outcome

1. Zero Change failure and security vulnerabilities.
2. reduce defect density matrix
3. One-piece flow, in sequence, on demand
4. Improved cycle time

What could a potential vision look like for a software development process? There is, of course, no right and wrong, and you need to develop your own for your context. Here is one potential vision:

- Zero defects
- Every check-in to production
- Highest value first, on demand
- Motivated people

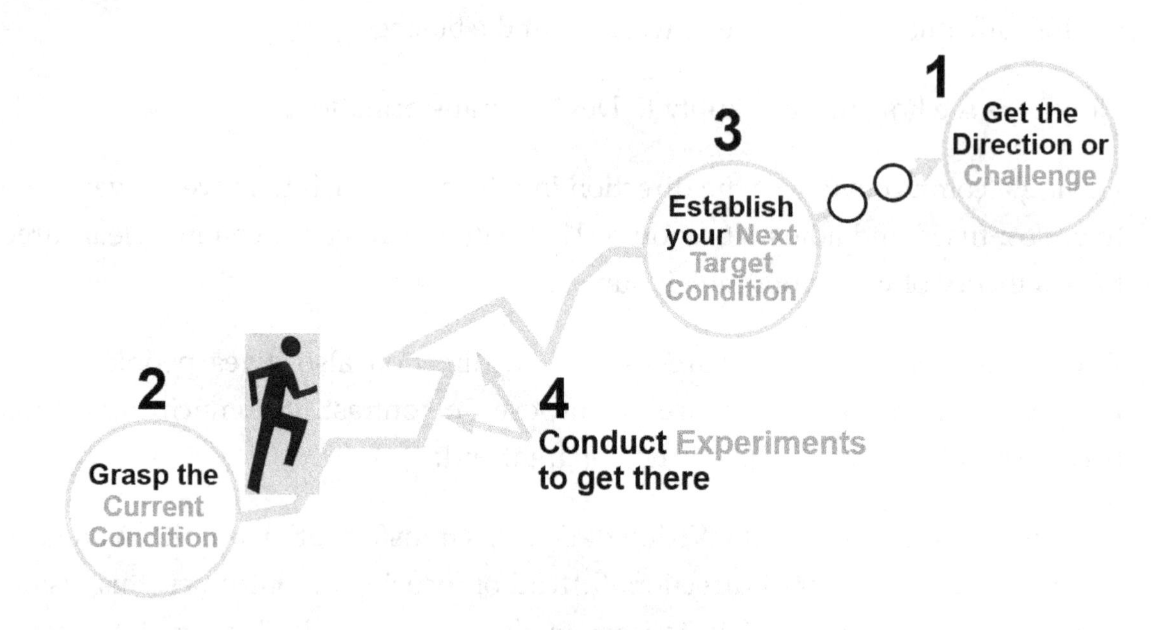

Source: Mike Rother

Understand the Current Situation

It's time to comprehend where you are right now after everyone is on the same page about your direction. You must develop a thorough awareness of the state of your operations right now. How exactly do you work? Describe your actual methods in detail. Instead of describing how you should work, describe how you do. A straightforward block representation of the many phases is typically preferable.

Additionally, gather process metrics that show how well your process works. Additionally, you want to begin gathering metrics for both processes and results. Process metrics describe your process's performance.

Process metrics such as Cycle time, WIP, Backlogs and Defects are frequently early warning systems that predict a process's result. On the other side, output metrics such as lead time and quality describe the operation's final product and outcome. These measurements were determined after the fact and are the outcome of our process management.

Establish the Next Target

It's time to outline your ideal state for the near future now that you clearly understand your direction and current condition. Establishing the following target condition is now necessary. When your process reaches the target state, you should have a Target Condition that describes how it should behave. The method should take precedence over the result. The process you follow should produce the desired result. A view that moves you closer to your vision should be the Target Condition. The view should be consistent with your operational approach and idea of what constitutes an improvement as part of your DevOps target.

By replicating the current condition, you can set a target condition. By doing this, you are comprising the output metrics, your process description, and the process metrics. Following that, you make a modification based on your view that will get you one step closer to realising your vision. Must express the target Condition in absolute rather than relative numbers. Whether you have attained the target condition or not should be crystal obvious.

A target condition's deadline is specified when it is set. Usually, the deadline is chosen one to three months in advance. It is best to select a deadline that will inspire you to get started right away. After that, the target conditions are over. Either you reach the target condition, or the deadline has passed.

Learning is heavily emphasised in both the Coaching Kata and the Improvement Kata. We better understand what might be an improvement as we learn more about how our processes operate. Set the Target Condition above your current level of expertise. It would be best if you were forced to think creatively. It ought to encourage you to attempt something new. Putting a square peg into a round hole should be how it feels. Creating a manageable target condition can help you avoid demotivating people. Try to adhere to the Goldilocks principle: Just Right is not too hard, nor too easy.

For process improvements to be successful, having a defined Target Condition is crucial. As a result, the organisation must wait until a target Condition is well-defined before beginning their improvement effort.

Once you discover the next target, you will need to perform PDCA towards your target.

Coaching Kata

The following essential aspect of Kata is coaching Kata. But first, let's see what coaching Kata is.

Coaching Kata is the second and essential element of the Kata model. The Coaching Kata supports the Improvement Kata by focusing on learning, improving, and heading correctly. The Improvement Kata's PDCA toward the Represents The ability, the fourth phase, is primarily supported by the Coaching Kata.

The coaching Kata usually has five questions. Such as

- What is the target condition?
- What is the status of the actual condition?
- What impedes to address of reaching the goal?
- What's next?
- What was learned and taken away?

In a Nutshell, Continuous improvement can be challenging. It requires an equally ongoing effort from all the members of your team. However, if you want to improve your daily habit, then Kata Model can significantly help. It helps automate repetition, streamline processes, and identify core routines that must be strictly adhered to. With Kata, you can set up a system where everyone in the organisation follows a consistent process to help the company achieve its goals.

PART 5 – MOKITAS IN THE MEASURE ROOM

CHAPTER 1: ACT ON KEY METRICS

Metrics: A quantitative assessment measure commonly used to assess, compare, and track performance or production.

DevOps is not a magic wand. You can wave over your software engineering team, IT department or company and expect magical transformations. Instead, it's a cultural shift requiring every team member's buy-in, primarily because DevOps focuses on streamlining the development process. Unfortunately, the outcomes of implementing DevOps can't be measured by how many times everyone high-fived or how many times you said "self-service." Likewise, you can't measure the value of DevOps with a straightforward metric. But that doesn't mean there aren't ways to measure its effectiveness at your organisation. This chapter explores different metrics for measuring your DevOps success and keeping tabs on it going forward.

What are DevOps metrics?

DevOps metrics are data points that show how well your engineers, development teams and organisation are performing. For example, DevOps metrics might measure the time it takes to get new features live. The number of bugs, how many releases you're doing per day. The number of broken features. Or the number of releases that go out without any error. DevOps metrics cover the entire process of software development, from ideation and the idea of creating a new feature to designing, building, testing, and deploying. DevOps metrics help you understand how your team is performing and where there is room for improvement.

What are critical DevOps metrics?

Regarding DevOps metrics, the three top critical metrics to measure are a lead time for changes, change failure rates and deployment frequency. Each of these metrics provides insight into whether your software delivery pipeline is efficient enough and whether any bottlenecks or issues impede the progress. The good news is that all three of these metrics are easy to track and don't require significant investment in new tools or software. For example, suppose you're measuring these three metrics and nothing else. In that case, you'll still understand how well your software delivery process operates. However, there are other DevOps metrics you can track as well to get a more holistic view of your organisation's efficiency.

Cycle Times: Cycle times show the time it takes for an engineer to go from the idea for a new feature to finishing the work and deploying it to production. For example, if it takes an engineer ten days to create a new feature that sends emails to the end users, cycle times would include the time it takes to ideate and designs the feature, write the code, test, and then deploy the feature to customers. There are a few different ways to measure cycle times. You can ask engineers to track their cycle times, calculate the average time it takes to finish projects or measure it based on tickets. Cycle times are an excellent way to measure progress and the efficiency of your team's work. If you're experiencing long cycle times, it might be due to a few things. For example, you could have too many open tickets or bugs that take too long to finish. Alternatively, your engineers may work on too many projects at once or need to use the correct practices to get projects done faster.

Defect Avoidance Rate: The defect avoidance rate is the percentage of defects you can avoid during the software development lifecycle. There are a few ways to calculate this. However, generally, you'll want to track defects and then figure out how many you would have had if you weren't following a DevOps process or methodology. For example, suppose you're following a DevOps approach. In that case, you might deploy code every couple of days, whereas a non-DevOps team might deploy code every few months. In this scenario, an engineer may find a bug in the code, fix it and ship it to customers. If you need to follow a DevOps process, that bug could get shipped to all customers. A defect avoidance rate formula would be the number of bugs you found in the iteration divided by the number of bugs you would have seen.

Deployment Frequency: As with many metrics, the deployment frequency metric is affected by several things. First, you'll want to measure how often you're releasing code to customers versus releasing it to staging. You'll also want to estimate how long it takes to release new code to users compared to releasing code to stage. Finally, you'll want to look at how often new features are being released compared to bug fixes how often are deployed. You can measure deployment frequency in a few ways: count the number of times you deploy code every day, week, or month. You can also look at the number of open tickets in the system for X amount of time. Alternatively, you can look at how long it's taking engineers to close out bugs and get code to production.

Mean Time to Recovery: The mean time to recovery metric shows how quickly your team can recover from issues. For example, suppose your web server goes down, and you're deploying code to fix the issue. In that case, the meantime to recovery is the time it takes your team (and, perhaps, the team that hosts your website) to fix the error and get everything back up and running. The mean time to recovery metric can also apply to how long your team takes to respond to a support request or deal with a critical bug. The mean time to recovery metric doesn't have any set-in-stone numbers, but it shows how quickly your team can respond to issues and get back up and running. For example, suppose the mean time to recovery metric is higher than it should be. In that case, something may be wrong with your software delivery pipeline or process.

What are Key Performance Indicators for Continuously Deploying Software?

Key performance indicators: or KPIs: are metrics that keep tabs on key business goals. KPIs apply to all businesses and can use in software engineering and DevOps. For example, if your company wants to double its revenue, you can follow KPIs to track how close you are to achieving that goal. In addition, some KPIs apply to the DevOps process: change failure rates, lead time for changes, mean time to recovery, defects, and cycle times. These metrics are essential for keeping tabs on the efficiency of your software delivery process and improving it whenever necessary.

Backlog Management Ratio (BMR): the ratio between the number of defects fixed and the number of defects submitted in a sprint/release. If this ratio exceeds the agreed value, the backlog of defects is increasing. If this is the case in successive releases, special efforts must make to eliminate the backlog. This is usually done by reducing new features for a sprint or devoting a sprint to bug fixing only.

Error rates: Tracking defect rates in your application is extremely important. They are not only an indicator of quality issues but also of ongoing performance and uptime issues. In addition, good best practices for handling exceptions are critical to good software.

Effectiveness of test cases: This is an index of the number of defects per 100 test cases executed. Choosing suitable test cases depends mainly on knowing the dependencies between the different modules and effective traceability metrics.

Defect density per module: this is another helpful metric that provides a measure of the vulnerability of the code for each module. It is the number of errors per module. Suppose the density is higher for a particular module. In this case, that module's coding quality needs to check, and the reasons for the errors need to investigate. Tracking such RCA would help reduce the density of errors per module.

Change error rate: Change error rates are a vital metric to assess the change's effectiveness. High-performing teams have change error rates of 0-10 per cent is healthier.

Ultimately, DevOps is about improving efficiency, reducing friction, and getting new features out more quickly. That means you need to track metrics that are important to those goals.

1. You face a backlog if your engineers take too long to write code.
2. You face a bottleneck if they spend too much time in code reviews.
3. If you're deploying code too frequently, you're putting customers at risk. If you need to deploy code more frequently.

In a Nutshell, you need to take advantage of the benefits of DevOps. Metrics are a great way to track all these factors and more. You can only expect to improve your software engineering process by keeping tabs on your current performance. Metrics are the easiest way to do that and identify improvement areas.

CHAPTER 2: MATURITY ASSESSMENT RITUAL

> **Maturity Assessment:** Evaluate an institution's processes to determine its ability to contribute consistently and continuously to achieving goals.

DevOps is a broad set of practices that help to streamline communication between software developers and IT operations teams. For DevOps to be successful, your company needs to have a high level of maturity in its principles. However, every company will flaw from the start. Furthermore, even companies that operate at a high level of DevOps maturity can hit roadblocks. Therefore, it's important to understand where your company stands so you can take the appropriate steps toward improvement. With this in mind, let's dive into why DevOps health-check and maturity assessment models are necessary for your company and how you can use them as an organisational tool.

What is a DevOps Health-check and Maturity Assessment Model?

A DevOps health check is a survey that allows you to analyse the current state of your DevOps practices. It enables you to understand where you stand organizationally by putting your current processes to the test. A health check assessment is critical to a maturity assessment because it allows you to get a baseline for where your company is. Ultimately, a health check acts as a measuring stick for you to use to show how your team can improve. A maturity assessment is a model that allows you to see how your team is performing in terms of DevOps. It's an in-depth analysis that gives your team a clear idea of what they need to improve on, where they stand organizationally, and what they can do to get to the next level.

Why is a DevOps Health-check and Maturity Assessment Model necessary?

A health check and maturity assessment model are necessary because they allow your team to reflect on the current state of your practices. They allow your team to evaluate their performance organizationally, which is crucial because it enables your team to see where they can improve. A health check and maturity assessment model allow your team to see how far they have come since the start. It will enable your team to celebrate their success, which is vital as it can help to generate a positive team culture. A health check and maturity assessment model can also use as a communication tool.

It allows your team to communicate with that outside of operations. Additionally, It will help you to provide an insight into how your procedures work and what the team can improve. This could be beneficial for several reasons. First, it allows your team to communicate their message to those unfamiliar with their organisation. It also allows that outside of your operations to see how your team operates, which can help to facilitate collaboration.

Why is a DevOps Maturity Assessment Important?

A DevOps maturity assessment is crucial because it allows your team to see where they stand organizationally. It will enable them to get a grip on where they can improve and where they excel. It will also allow your team members to see how their organisation can improve their procedures in terms of efficiency and quality. It enables those outside your organisation to clearly understand what they can expect. It allows them to see how your company runs and how their role can fit into the operational model. It can also help organisations to obtain funding for projects and initiatives. A DevOps maturity assessment can also use as a benchmark for organisations. It allows other companies to see how your company runs, what to expect, and how to foster their own culture better.

Levels of DevOps Maturity Assessment Model

Every initiative and transformation can help best asses with some degree of maturity assessment. So, DevOps. But the real challenge is that most organisations need to perform the proper maturity assessment. There are a few reviews to be applied at every stage of your processes, such as planning, coding, CI/CD, Release, DevOps CALMS Model and operational metrics. So, let's table the assessment here. These are fundamental steps for constructing a DevOps Maturity Assessment Model.

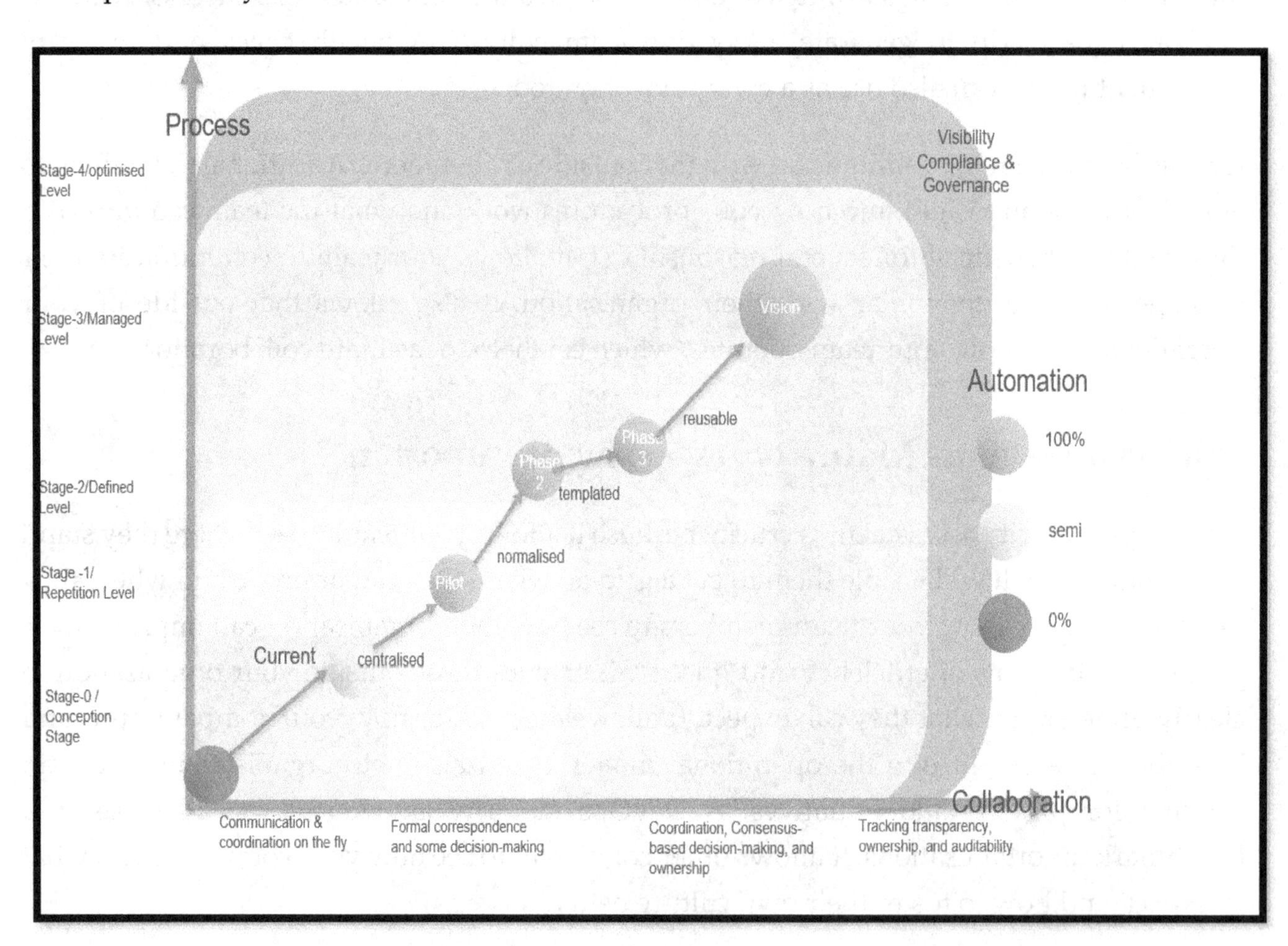

Stage-0 /Conception Stage: In the early stages, the organisation may still need to be aware of DevOps and its potential benefits. Therefore, the organisation must start from scratch. Organisations at this stage follow waterfall project management - lengthy approval and change processes and teams structured around a capability for their IT projects. They plan and design everything up front before development teams start coding. When everything is ready, separate teams deliver the application to production. Testing begins very late in the process. Likely, they do not apply the concepts of shift-left safety.

For operations, a separate team is waiting for developers to hand over their applications with a thick manual with instructions on how to deploy them. Missing data and miscommunication characterise handing over the new version and associated deployment information and finger-pointing when things go wrong. For some organisations, an initial DevOps stage can be overwhelming. However, they can also benefit the most when someone at the executive level decides to take action to solve the problem.

Stage 1/ Repetition Level: At this level, organisations know the core principles of DevOps and apply them in their daily work. Environments and their configurations are versioned and can be set up consistently. They are on the right track to facilitate collaboration between development and operations. Changes do not come as a surprise, but they are well communicated.

Organisations working at this level are not just "reactive" to whatever comes their way. They are proactive and work toward repeatable processes for the areas they understand well. However, teams tend to deliver relatively large features requiring more work to manage and test. Breaking more extensive services into smaller microservices remains a challenge. Operations teams must manually intervene when things go wrong in production.

Stage 2/Defined Level: a vital feature of this level is consistency across domains and themes. Processes are repeatable but also standardised. For example, database changes are made automatically with each release, non-production deployments are rolled out automatically, and monitoring is built into each application. Integration tests are run automatically and serve as quality control for each subsequent stage in the delivery pipeline.

Teams are organised by project or product rather than by skill set. Development teams work toward implementing precise requirements that deliver clear business value. All processes are communicated to all stakeholders, and documentation and release notes are automatically generated.

Stage 3/Managed Level: All environments are effectively managed at the managed level. Database changes and rollbacks are self-tested with each iteration of the product. The delivery process is predictable and runs regularly. Therefore, stakeholders know what to expect and when to expect it. Applications are actively monitored in production, and metrics are collected.

Teams know how to incorporate feedback into the next iteration. The company uses a knowledge management tool to capture existing knowledge and provide additional expertise to the team—DevOps Coaches coach the teams to move them forward. The culture is not a bottleneck and welcomes change to achieve company goals.

Stage 4/Optimised Level: At the optimised level, processes are fully automated, and testing is done on the store floor. They know how to deal with issues like overloaded systems. The system itself scales or adapts to peak demands. It also adapts to potential problems such as network interruptions or other infrastructure failures.

How to Create a DevOps Health-check and Maturity Assessment Model?

The first step toward creating a health check and maturity assessment model is to determine what aspects of the model you want to focus on. Building a DevOps Health-check and Maturity Assessment Model is

crucial because it helps to guide your team on what factors to focus on and how to improve. Once you have determined what you want to focus on, you need to conduct surveys. You want to perform surveys with your team members and those outside of your operation to get feedback on how they perceive your organisational procedures. You want to survey those familiar with your organisation to get feedback and suggestions on improvement. You also want to explore those unfamiliar with your DevOps and operational procedures; this will help you get their advice and input on improving. Once you have completed the surveys, it's time to analyse them. The data you receive will help you pinpoint better what your team needs to improve and how to facilitate those improvements. It will allow you better to create a health check and maturity assessment model.

Steps to Developing Your Company's DevOps Maturity Model

The first step to developing a company's DevOps maturity model is to create a health check and maturity assessment model. Once you have completed this, it's time to understand where your team stands. Next, it's time to analyse the data and determine what your team needs to improve and where they excel. Finally, once you have completed this, it's time to communicate with the team and those outside the operation.

You were once completing communications such as meetings and other forms of collaboration. Creating an action plan and translating those action items into your Tracking list is encouraged. That allows your team to improve on those aspects they need to improve on while maintaining and excelling in the areas they do well. It's also important to celebrate your success and the successes of your team members. Finally, maintaining a positive team culture is essential, so everyone feels supported and appreciated. With these steps in mind, you can better develop a company's DevOps maturity model.

What Can You Learn from a DevOps Health Check?

A DevOps health check and maturity assessment model can teach you much about your organisation and how to improve. One of the best things you can learn from a health check and maturity assessment model is that it allows you to see what areas you excel in and where you can improve. It lets you see where your strengths lie and which operations need improvement. It allows you to create an action plan to focus on improving those areas that need improvement while maintaining the sites that perform well. Finally, it will enable you to create a clear strategy for your team to see where improvements need to be. And how their roles can help to facilitate those improvements.

In a Nutshell, A health check and maturity assessment model are essential aspects of any organisation's DevOps practices. They allow your team to reflect on the current state of their operational procedures. And get a better idea of how well they are performing, and see where they can improve. A health check and maturity assessment model can also use as a communication tool that allows outside team members to get a better idea of how your operations work.

CHAPTER 3: OBJECTIVES AND KEY RESULTS A SMART WAY TO ASSES DEVOPS PROGRESSION

Objectives and Key Results (OKRs): A metric that defines guild and team "objectives" as well as the measurable "key results" that describe each objective's achievement.

Objectives and Key Results, commonly known as OKRs, are processes used to set and track specific objectives for an organisation. This framework helps measure a company's success in reaching its long-term vision. In this chapter, you will find step-by-step instructions on implementing Objectives and Key Results (OKRs) at your company or organisation. If your company is ready to stand out from others and make the most of 2019, these tips will help you succeed. Operating a business can sometimes be overwhelming, which is why some companies prefer a structured approach to management. Objectives and Key Results (OKRs) can take some of the stress away from running a business because it's a simple system that anyone can understand.

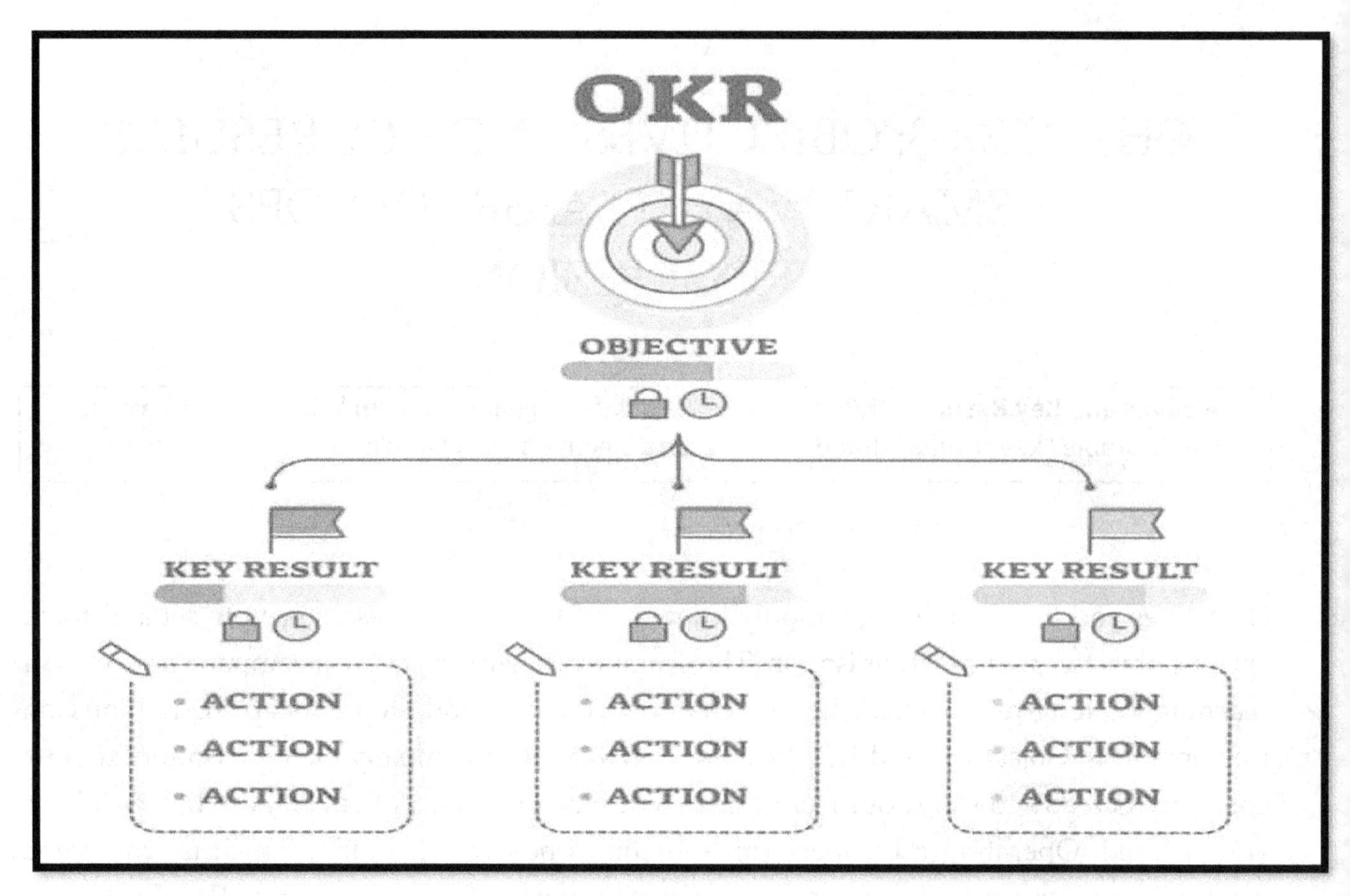

Source: businessanalystmentor

What are the Objectives and Key Results?

Generally, objectives are the overarching goals a company aims to achieve over a while. Typically, these objectives focus on the bigger picture of the business, such as increasing revenue or the number of customers. Objectives are like the big fish you want to catch, while key results are the smaller fish you see while trying to catch the big fish. Key results are the individual tasks needed to meet a company's objectives.

Now let us look at the few benefits of the OKR Model.

Benefits of OKR

As you know, Objective and key results, or OKRs, are a system for setting goals and measuring progress. They are popular in Silicon Valley and other tech companies for aligning teams around company objectives.

The idea behind OKRs is that they provide a way to measure progress toward company goals and individual objectives. This is the easier way to see how everyone contributes to the company's success.

There are many benefits of using OKRs in the workplace:

1. They help employees focus on what needs to be accomplished
2. They make it easier to set goals and measure progress.
3. They help employees identify priorities and develop better strategies.
4. They keep managers informed about what their team is doing.

While skimming the benefits briefly, I will list here a few benefits that make advantages to the entire DevOps Ecosystems in your organisation.

Few benefits of using OKRs:

1. Align your employees with the goals of your company.
2. Communicate the organisation's expectations to every individual or team without ambiguity.
3. Focus on your goals to increase productivity.
4. Track progress towards goals
5. You make many decisions at work, and the outcomes can be favorable for you with correct information. Making wise and informed decisions is essential.
6. Achieve measurement, accountability, and transparency.
7. Use regular weekly updates to gain vision and insight, which will help to make decisive actions.

8. See how goal progress aligns with the company's vision, strategy, and top priorities.
9. Be effective in setting clear and specific goals.
10. Use OKR to prioritise tasks and be more accountable when achieving your goals.
11. By setting goals and making progress towards them, individuals can experience higher engagement levels than those without goals.
12. Ensure a company-wide sense of insight and transparency by starting with individual teams
13. Analyse the underlying causes of why an individual did not achieve their goals
14. Aids to assist better resource allocation and management.
15. Capture cross-functional dependencies across teams.

Now, look at how to write OKR.

How to write OKRs

OKRs are a great way to set intentions for your company and can achieve with this formula:

For objectives to be powerful, they need to be clear, inspiring, and easy for People must understand the goal at first sight. To achieve this, goals should be clear, inspiring, and easy to understand. The golden rule when writing goals is that any reasonable person should be able to accept your goal quickly.

To help you reach your goals, you could ask these questions:

- Every member of an individual's team, department and company should have only a few objectives limit of 3-5 per level.
- Do they have measurable, tangible goals? For example, if a sales team was responsible for an order, they should be entitled to the resources needed to fill it. However, it is just somebody's job to sell a product. In that case, they might not be responsible for shipping it, so you'd expect them to manage just their commitments. In addition, company-wide goals also require management to keep them on track. We could do this by answering questions or through reporting and accountability. With this accountability, goals are actionable.

- The best way to determine whether something should remain at an enterprise level okay is to think, "Why do we need to care about these specific objectives?" Objectives should have high value and have easily measurable results. If someone cannot see its value, it is best to reconsider it.

The best way to test the validity of an idea is to ask yourself: "Why should anyone care?" Questions like "What's in it for me?" or "Is this valuable?" will help you determine if that idea has potential. A proper goal would have high value and be easily measurable. It's crucial to look at your concept turns every which way and make sure that.

Key results determine success. Any reasonable person would agree that reaching the key result means accomplishing the objective.

When defining key results, make sure to state them clearly - and where possible, give measurable goals instead of binary outcomes. Doing so makes it easier for you to track your success and see how much you've been able to achieve.

Every organisation needs measurable objectives. So, it's essential to carry out a key result analysis on your goals and ensure they will help you achieve what's most important. First, ask yourself these questions about your objectives:

Results are going to vary from team to team. You want to ensure your employees are manageable so that your metrics are manageable. You must have objectives, but review key results for general effectiveness first.

Is your objective focused on achieving the RESULT or what you need to accomplish to complete it? For example, a company may want to improve conversion rates by 20% as a key result. Improving conversion rates can be done by various methods, such as improving the design of one's online store or changing the content on one's website, depending on the constraints.

Is your team or company challenging themselves and striving for new things? If not, you'll find that achieving business as usual is not enough. You want better results, don't you?

The targets must be realistic. Achieving them can help you succeed. The goal is to set more ambitious, not set unrealistic ones. it should involve the following bullet points

- How will the responsibility be assigned?
- Who needs to do what?
- What resources do they need to get it done?
- Thinking about your company's goals and brainstorming with your team before selecting them is essential.

Considering the above-bulleted lists will get them fired up and invested in their work. They'll be excited and more motivated when they see the result of these efforts.

When creating key results for each objective, use sticky notes or a collaboration tool to have each team member offer suggestions. Then, share and debate with one another until you find a good difficulty level.

When brainstorming, it's important to allow team members the freedom to give and share their input when considering objectives and key results. That's why we strive to provide an encouraging and supportive environment where they're comfortable expressing themselves.

- In our last chapter, we skimmed about KPIs; it is worth looking at the differences between OKR and KPIs.

OKRs vs KPIs

There is a slight overlap between the two; each serves its function: OKRs are for strategy, and KPIs are for metrics.

OKR and KPI differences

Despite their apparent similarities, there are several differences between KPIs and OKRs.

- OKRs are linked to strategic goals, while KPIs are linked to processes.
- OKR is real-time, while KPI is Lagging.
- Cross-functionality is one of the key benefits of using OKRs. They can help show how related initiatives cooperate and demonstrate that every business benefits. KPIs only focus on singular aspects of your business, so you might miss essential factors about your company.
- Flexibility: OKRs change as strategy evolves, while KPIs remain constant.
- Nature of design: OKRs are inherently focused, while KPIs cover the entire organisation.
- Visibility: OKRs are transparent by default, while KPIs are constrained to the line of business.
- Longevity: OKRs typically change each quarter, while KPIs tend to maintain
- Incentivisation: OKRs follow more constraints than KPIs, which can be gamified.
- Hierarchy: OKRs support one another, while KPIs are flat and share equal importance.
- Scale: OKRs are a management tool, while KPIs are used within a management tool.

Create the right environment for success

It's essential to create an environment where employees are encouraged to try new things and can expand their skills. You can do this by making sure that the structure of your OKRs is flexible but also tight enough. It should be challenging but also achievable. To do this, you should communicate your objectives and key results with your employees. If there is a problem with the flow of information, it can be a massive setback to your company's success. It would be good to encourage employees to experiment with new ideas and solutions to problems. While meeting your company's objectives is crucial, you should promote creativity and problem-solving skills to prepare employees for the future.

Define what success means to your company

This may seem like a no-brainer, but defining what success means to your company is essential. What are the goals of your organisation? What are the long-term and short-term objectives, and how will you measure their success? This information is necessary to create goals that will help your company succeed. An excellent way to perform this is to create a SWOT analysis. Usually, SWOT analysis will help you understand your company's strengths, weaknesses, opportunities, and threats. You can use this information to create goals and objectives that will take your company to the next level. You can also ask for customer feedback if you need help improving your company. It's essential to listen to what they say, and you'll be able to use this information to create objectives and goals to improve your company.

Establish company-wide objectives

Once you've established what your company will achieve, it's time to create the objectives to help you succeed. Create a list of objectives, and assign each to the members of your organisation. Doing so will ensure that everybody is on the same page and understands what they need to accomplish. It's essential to be realistic with the objectives that you create. An overly ambitious set of objectives won't benefit your company and will only set you up for failure. Your objectives should be challenging but realistic. If you need help with objectives, you can use the SMART acronym to guide you. SMART stands for Specific, Measurable, Attainable, Realistic, and Timely.

Create individual objectives

Once you've established company-wide objectives, it's time to move to the individual objectives of your employees. Create a list of objectives for each person on your team, and ensure they know what they must accomplish throughout the year. These objectives should align with the company objectives, so they can easily combine to create one complete OKRs.

It's essential to make sure that your objectives are challenging but still realistic. If you set realistic objectives, your employees will stay caught up and likely fail before the year ends. Remember that you can constantly adjust the objectives as time goes on.

Establish your key results for each objective

After you've established company-wide objectives and individual objectives, it's time to create the key results for each objective. This is the final phase in setting up your OKR framework, so you should be ready to plunge into this part. When you're creating key results, make sure that they are measurable. You want to be able to track the progress of your key results so that you can adjust your strategy if needed. You can also create more than one key result for each objective. This will give you more options when tracking progress and allow you to be more flexible with your strategy.

Measure Outcomes and Set Dates

The next step in setting up your OKRs framework is to measure the outcomes. Measuring outcomes will allow you to track the progress of your key results and ensure that they're reaching your desired outcomes. You can use spreadsheets and other tracking methods to measure the outcomes of each objective. Once you've added all your key results to your spreadsheets, you can see progress. This will allow you to adjust your strategy if you notice that your key results need to catch up or if they need to meet the proper outcomes. Your key results should be reviewed and adjusted as time goes on. If you need help to reach your goals, you should re-evaluate your key results and try to find ways to improve them. This will allow you to achieve your objectives even faster.

Choose 3-5 key results in your DevOps.

Once you've established company-wide and individual objectives, it's time to create key results for each. You can achieve many things to improve your organisation and reach your goals. First, however, you need to choose the right objectives and key outcomes to provide your company with the highest value. Once you've established your key results, you can use them to create your timeline. You can set dates for each of your key results and track the progress that you're making towards achieving them. This will allow you to easily see if your employees are meeting their key results and are on track to attain their objectives. When setting your key results for your DevOps journey, ensure they're measurable and align with your objectives. You can use the SMART method to ensure that your key results fit the bill.

Set measurable objectives for each key result in your DevOps Journey

Once you've established company-wide and individual objectives, it's time to create key results for each. You can achieve things to improve your organisation and reach your goals. First, however, you need to choose the right key results that will bring the most value to your company. Once you've established your objectives and key results, you can set a timeline for each. You can also track the progress that you're making towards achieving them and see if your employees are meeting their key results. This will allow you to easily see if your employees are on track to attain their objectives.

Celebrate your wins

Keeping track of the wins your team accomplishes over the year is essential. Then, celebrate your successes and encourage your employees to do even better in the future. You can use Whiteboards, rewards systems spreadsheets and other tracking methods to keep track of your wins. You can also create a board to celebrate your successes visually. Encouragement will help you stay motivated and encourage your employees to do better. Keeping track of your wins is essential because it will show you what works and doesn't work for your company. In addition, this information will be helpful when you're creating objectives and key results for the following year.

CHAPTER 4: OPERATIONAL INTELLIGENCE PLATFORM

Operational intelligence (OI): An information analysis technique that enables decisions and action items in business and technology operations to be based on real-time data generated or collected by an institution.

Operational intelligence (or Operational Analytics) is a tool or technique used to help businesses optimise their processes and better understand the "why-why" of performance rather than just a snapshot of the current result. It's about identifying inefficiencies, problems, and other issues in your business. So, you can take swift action and correct any problems before they become more significant hardships. Operational intelligence is beneficial for any business because it helps detect issues faster and respond more quickly.

It enables enterprises to move from traditional metrics to predictive analytics to identify risks before they become significant problems. It also provides insights that allow you to target customers with the right products at the right time.

In this chapter, we will flip thru the Value of Operational Intelligence and Why It Is Beneficial to any business. Then, here is further insight into why operational intelligence benefits an organisation.

Before looking at the benefits, it will make more sense to look at the critical features of the OI. Eventually, every organisation will yield numerous benefits from these features of OI Stacks.

What are the critical features of operational intelligence?

Real-time monitoring: Real-time monitoring is the core of what OI (Operational Intelligence) is all about. Every OI solution will monitor data in real-time to understand what the situation is right now. So, whether it's sensitive data, sales analytics, or alerts and enable, the organisation has visibility and response options at their fingertips. In addition, OI provides real-time analytics and alerts that update in seconds and avoid laborious troubleshooting.

Dashboards and visualisations: One benefit of OI is its ability to digest many data points and present them in a summarised, intuitive format. Dashboards are the primary mechanism for this and can give this information visually for easy understanding.

OI systems are powerful tools and almost infinitely customisable. The same must be true for dashboards to cater to different people's needs. For example, A financial advisor and a product developer rely on the information. However, they will receive different insights from their dashboards. Therefore, in any OI Tool, the dashboard and data visualisations are ideally customisable so that the organisation can understand the exact information that's important to the organisation.

Real-time alerting techniques: Operational intelligence doesn't just ensure that your systems are running smoothly. It also alerts when something significant happens and aids incident and problem management Teams significantly in ITSM organisation. As a result, an organisation can avoid false alarms with greater flexibility in tweaking the configurations and other settings. For example, you can adjust its settings to trigger notifications only when important events occur. Here's another time that automation helps. Bots alert you before an event, giving you time to react and address the problem before it escalates.

How Does Operational Intelligence Work?

The process of operational intelligence starts with getting the correct data into your business analytics system. Then, you build models and act based on the insights that come from the data. In a manufacturing company, for example, operational intelligence will give you insights into your supply chain. You can see how long the supply chain is taking and determine the most efficient route for your products. Once you have the data, you can build models to forecast future trends, such as demand and product sales, based on current trends. Once you have operational intelligence, you can optimise your processes and provide better customer experiences. In addition, you can gain insights into the following areas:

Customer experience: Customer experience (CE) is your customers' journey through your business and how they interact with you. You can use operational intelligence to understand your customers' journey. Areas of opportunities. And where they are getting stuck or where they may be having issues. You can also use it to understand better how customers prefer to interact with you, such as through digital channels.

Product and service insights: - Product and service insights are your understanding of the products and services you offer. You can use this data to determine how your products and services are performing and identify where you can make improvements.

How do you get started with operational intelligence?

Before implementing operational intelligence, you should determine your business goals and ensure that the solution meets your needs. It would help if you provided that the answer is easy to use and has the right integrations for your data. Next, you need to collect data, such as customer information, product information, inventory data, and any other relevant data that can help you understand your business. You can collect this data from multiple systems and sources, such as your existing business intelligence tool, customer relationship management system, or product management system. Once you have collected your data, you can build models and gain insights into your business. You can also use your operational intelligence solution to collaborate more effectively with your team members by sharing insights and visualisations.

How do you choose the best operational intelligence solution/tools?

When choosing an operational intelligence solution, you should ensure that it is easy to use and integrates with your existing data sources. You also must ensure that it provides the insights you need, such as insights into your customers and their journey, supply chain, or product and service performance. Your operational intelligence solution should also be able to scale with your business as it grows. This means it should be able to handle the amount of data you are storing and quickly make decisions from this data. It would be best if you chose an easy operational intelligence solution to implement and use. It should have an intuitive user interface and enable you to collaborate with your team members. It should also can connect with your existing data sources, such as your current business intelligence tool, customer relationship management system, or product management system.

Benefits of Operational Intelligence

Upon implementing the Operational intelligence platforms, organisations will yield benefits; here are a few.

Business Insights: Operational intelligence solutions enable you to get the right insights from your data to act on them. It provides a holistic view of your business, including information on your customers, products, and supply chain.

Collaboration: With operational intelligence, you can integrate data from multiple systems and sources to provide a real-time view of your business that is accessible to everyone. Which will allow the teams to collaborate more effectively and take swift action as needed.

Predictive analytics: Predictive analytics uses historical data to forecast future trends. Operational intelligence solutions enable you to use predictive analytics to identify risks, such as supply-chain issues before they become significant problems.

Speed to value: Operational intelligence solutions provide the momentum to the value needed in today's business world. You can get up and running with the answer quickly, and it is easy to use, which means you can begin to see results and benefits much faster.

Increase Efficiency and Productivity: The data you receive from operational intelligence software can help you determine the areas of opportunity. For example, where there are too many employees working or too much inventory. You can use this data to take corrective action and increase employee productivity.

Provide Greater Visibility into Business: You can use operational intelligence to get a holistic view of your business, such as your customers, products, and supply chain. This allows you to see how your business's different parts fit together.

PART 6 – MOKITAS IN THE SHARING AND SUSTAIN ROOM

CHAPTER 1: SITE RELIABILITY ENGINEERING

Site Reliability Engineering: Principles and practises that embody aspects of software engineering and apply them to information technology infrastructure and operations.

Welcome to Part six of this book. Usually, In the DevOps CALMS Framework, S stands for Sharing, But I would differ. S for Sustainability will need sustainable achievements as every DevOps Transformation success. To measure the achievements, we need to have various metrics. In the DevOps Journey, Sharing is coming across everywhere. We should open ourselves to sharing metrics. The "S" in the CALMS Framework must need to look at with a big lens that is nothing but Site reliability. What is the use of DevOps without 99.99% uptime of any services in your Organisation? Due to the principle's similarities of the Site Reliability Engineering. The Organisation is often biased by ignoring the SRE discipline. This chapter will explain how SRE and DevOps can work together to support your business's DevOps transformation. in fact, it would be a good idea for you to accommodate SRE as a discipline in your DevOps transformation.

DevOps transformation is no longer something that just software companies should think about. The modern business world is changing fast, and to stay relevant as a company, you need to find ways for your business to meet the needs of customers in digital spaces rather than physical ones. If you've read anything about DevOps or SRE in the last few years, you might think they've sworn enemies locked in an eternal battle for control of your production environment. But with the right approach, both can work together to support your business's DevOps transformation. We'll clarify how these concepts can help your transformation and business success, why they need to understand their roles within the team, and how they can best work together to support your transformation journey success.

What is Site Reliability Engineering?

Site reliability engineering (SRE) is a computer science field focusing on software systems' availability and resilience. The main goal of SRE is to ensure that systems are available and responsive to users' needs. SRE teams use various techniques to achieve this, including proactive monitoring, alerting, toil reduction, and chaos engineering.

SRE is a discipline that is highly aware of incentives and their impacts, but it is also largely mute on issues like information silos and barriers. Nevertheless, due to the business case and the enhanced operational procedures involved, it would assist CI and CD. In another sense, SRE and DevOps share common beliefs for slightly different causes.

SRE teams use various techniques to ensure that systems are available and responsive to users' needs. These techniques include proactive monitoring, alerting, toil reduction, and chaos engineering.

Proactive monitoring is a technique SRE teams use to identify potential issues before they cause outages. By monitoring system performance and health indicators, SREs can detect problems early and take corrective action before user's impact.

Alerting is another technique used by SRE teams to ensure availability. By setting up alerts, we can proactively avoid service disruptions and painful downtimes,

Also, SRE is a discipline that focuses on efficiently running systems. One of the critical concepts in SRE is the error budget. An error budget measures how much downtime a system can tolerate while still meeting its SLAs. They allow for a certain amount of errors in a system. This allows for a more efficient system, as it can tolerate specific errors without affecting the overall performance.

Toil reduction is another important concept in SRE. Toil is the term used to describe the work required to keep a system running. For example, manual tasks that could automate are toil.

Toil reduction seeks to reduce the work needed to keep a system running. We can do this through automation and simplification.

Proactive monitoring and alerting an essential aspect of SRE. Monitoring the system closely can detect and address potential problems before they cause downtime. Aggressive monitoring techniques it is easy to see potential issues before they occur. By monitoring the system closely, SRE can identify potential issues and take steps to prevent them from becoming actual problems.

Chaos engineering is another important concept in SRE. This is deliberately injecting faults into a system to test its resilience. By doing this, SRE teams can identify and fix potential problems before they cause actual outages. Chaos engineering is a technique to introduce errors into a system to test its resilience deliberately. This allows for a more robust system, as it can identify and correct problems before they cause significant issues.

SRE can be a valuable partner for DevOps teams. By working together, the two disciplines can yield maximum benefits. DevOps teams can provide code development and deployment expertise, while SRE teams can efficiently run systems. The two disciplines can create a powerful force for change by combining their skills.

How Can SRE be Associated with DevOps?

It's a set of practices and tools that help organisations run large-scale distributed systems effectively. The focus is to ensure that all customers receive 99.99% uptime and that none of them experiences any significant service interruptions. SRE was initially created at Google and has since been adopted by other companies like LinkedIn and Netflix. Some experts say SRE will soon become a mainstream delivery model for enterprise-level software.

SRE is often associated with DevOps, but the two are different. DevOps is focused on bringing together the entire software development lifecycle and automating it as much as possible. SRE, on the other hand, is focused on how you run the production systems behind those applications. As a result, SRE teams have many of the same responsibilities as DevOps teams. Still, they also have a few unique responsibilities, like making sure that the systems they run are scalable, reliable, and able to meet high uptime SLOs.

SRE vs DevOps – how are they different?

Both fields require engineering, but the skillset required is slightly different. The core goal of an SRE engineer is to deliver reliable and robust engineering solutions. An SRE engineer strongly focuses on reducing risk, improving reliability, and preventing outages. While SREs strongly emphasise operational excellence, they typically focus on something other than building new features or products. On the other hand, DevOps engineers focus more on the product's entire lifecycle and collaboration between cross-functional teams. Another critical difference between DevOps and SRE is that DevOps is a philosophy, whereas SRE is a set of tools and processes.

SRE vs DevOps: Which Productivity Approach is Better?

It takes much work to conclude the productivity of the two methodologies, as the success of both methods depends upon the Organisation in which the entire delivery approach is implemented. However, it's possible to understand the benefits of both techniques with a few examples. If you're working in an organisation struggling with scalability, availability, and inconsistency, SRE can help get you back on track. If you have an organisation that needs to be aligned with the business goals, SRE can help bring everyone to the same page. These are just a few examples of how SRE can help you get out of a rut and get on track with your and digital transformation. If you're already on your digital transformation and have a high level of consistency and scalability, then implementing DevOps can help you scale even further. You can enforce practices like microservices and continuous delivery to scale your development efforts even further.

Some essential concepts of SRE

SLOs - Service Level Objectives: When customers use your product, they expect a certain level of performance. For example, they expect the application to be online and available 99.99% of the time. SLOs are the key metrics that determine if your application meets your customers' needs.

Error budget: Error budgets are a way to set expectations with customers. What percentage of downtime is acceptable? How many errors can you expect? What does "typical" look like? These are all questions that error budgets help determine.

Toil reduction: Efforts like toil reduction are to minimise the work required to maintain your systems. Manual labour is error-prone, expensive, and can be incredibly tedious.

What are SRE Best practices?

Automate everything: It should be automated if you can automate a task. This is an essential concept for SRE teams to follow. It ensures that manual jobs are eliminated and can consistently apply a repeatable process to all systems.

SLO Metrics: This is a no-brainer, but make sure you have metrics to track your SLOs. These metrics will help you make necessary adjustments and prevent significant outages.

Make everything idempotent: Idempotency is the ability to change systems or data and expect the same result every time. For example, if you're dealing with a database, inserting a row into the database once should only be inserted once, no matter how many times the request is made.

Make everything discoverable: If you make changes to your system, make sure the documentation is updated. If you're using a tool like GitHub, follow the best practices, like making PRs for changes and using good commit messages.

Proactively monitor SLOs: Metrics should reflect and predict the SLOs throughout the entire lifecycle of a product. - SLO Metrics are crucial and critical for seeing how your application is behaving and identifying potential issues in the system. Use tools like Datadog, Sensu, or New Relic to proactively monitor your SLOs.

Why is SRE essential for DevOps transformation?

The DevOps transformation aims to unify the entire delivery pipeline and help teams become more effective. SRE can facilitate this transformation by bringing order to chaos, providing guidance on best practices, and helping teams work together more efficiently. For example, implementing tools to track and agree with measure metrics in your DevOps Journey across the entire Organisation would be best. SRE can help you do just that. In addition, SRE can help bring order to the chaos by implementing tools like monitoring and metrics across the Organisation. This will allow you to see how your application is behaving and identify potential issues in the system.

How SRE and DevOps can work together to support your Organisation's transformation

SRE and DevOps provide unique benefits to help your business transform along the digital journey. While SRE brings order to chaos, providing best practices and implementing monitoring metrics, DevOps helps create a culture of collaboration between engineering teams. When these two groups work together, they can streamline processes, automate tedious tasks, and help your business meet the needs of customers in digital spaces rather than physical ones. If you want to take your business transformation to the next level, these two teams must communicate with each other. They bring something unique to the table, and when they work together, they can help your business run more efficiently and meet customers' needs in digital spaces.

In a Nutshell, you must embrace DevOps transformation if your company wants to succeed in the modern business landscape. However, transformation requires a significant change in how your Organisation operates, and it's often a big challenge. Thankfully, the two concepts of SRE and DevOps can help make this transition much more manageable. In this chapter, we've explained what SRE is and how it can help your business succeed. We've also covered how SRE can work with DevOps to support your business's digital transformation.

PART 7 – MOKITAS MODERNISATION PROCESS OF DEVOPS

CHAPTER 1: MODERNISATION OF SOURCE CODE MANAGEMENT

Monorepo: A Single repository that contains multiple projects with clearly defined relationships.

While organisations are embarking on DevOps Journey, it is worth reconciling the current SCM strategies and flows. New software release processes and DevOps principles have shifted the focus of software development from managing individual software packages to keeping track of entire application modules. This has led to increased adoption of Software Configuration Management (SCM) tools and new practices better equipped for handling modern software development scenarios. As in the fast phase of faster to market. Operating a successful software release process is challenging, especially when many factors must be considered. This chapter will explore some of the primary challenges with SCM processes and how you can address them in your organisation. Read on to learn more. For Example, Branching strategies, a Faster release process, and, most notably, Monorep. Let me introduce Monorep if you have yet to come across it.

If you're currently in the software development space or have ever dipped your toes into it, chances are you've heard the term "monorepo" before. Every other day, another article pops up about how a company has adopted a new type of organisational structure or how some company has switched to something else. If you need clarification and wondering what a monorepo is, keep reading. This chapter will explain why this monorep is becoming increasingly popular among software developers.

Let us look at Branching strategies first.

What are Software Branches?

A branch is a copy of a code base maintained in a version control system. Branching helps software development teams to work in parallel. It separates "work in progress" from tested and stable code.

Branches allow development teams to work together within a central code base. When a developer creates a branch, the version control system creates a copy of the code base. Changes to the branch do not affect other developers on the team. This is a good thing because features under development can cause instabilities that would be very disruptive if all the work was in the main codebase. But branches do not have to live in solitary confinement. Developers can easily pull changes from other developers to collaborate on features and ensure their private branch stays within the main branch.

What are Branching strategies Aiming to Achieve?

1. Enables developers to create workflows that lead to structured releases
2. Enables parallel development and faster release cycles
3. Streamlines developer workflow without adding overhead.
4. Integrates efficiently with all DevOps practices and tools

What are the best Branching strategies?

Well, there are no straightforward answers to this question. It is derived based on your product, the nature of the application or product development, and Compliance and regulation requirements, especially banking and financial sectors. The nature of your organisation model and many other surrounding processes involve it. But in agile and DevOps, transformed organisations, are focused on branching models as simple as x and y. So, let us See what is x, and What is y?

x is the primary branch, such as are Development Master, Release and Development branches. At the same time, y is the supporting branch, such as the Features branch, Bug fixes and Hotfixes. The primary branches focus on Production release thru staging branches, such as the development branch. In contrast, supporting branches focus on the development phases.

Let's look take a brief look.

Master or Main Branch: The primary branch is where all the production code is stored. in other words, it's a golden source of truth repository. Once the code in the 'development branch' is ready for release, the changes are merged into the main branch and used for deployment.

Development: The branch where actual development work is carrying. All pre-produced code is stored here. The finished code from all supporting branches is merged directly into the development branch.

Feature: Feature branches are mainly used to develop new features and addition off exclusively from the development branch.

Hotfix: These branches are used for production problems that need to fix quickly. They can branch from the master or main branch but must merge into the master and development branches. Otherwise, code breaks are inevitable in development branches for future releases.

Release: This branch combines corrections and improvements and prepares the production release. It is branched off from the development branch and merged with the development and master branches.

Well, that's about branching strategies. The above-listed branching mechanisms are mainly suitable for organisations in brownfield development environments and monolithic architectural ecosystems.

Now it's time to look for entirely green field development organisations such as microservices, Micro front end, modern web, and mobile development fashion. Usually, in such environments, Monorepo is an excellent suggestion to consider

What Is a Monorepo?

A monorepo is an organisational structure in which all project code is stored and managed in one location. In addition, A monorepo is a single repository containing several projects with clearly defined relationships made up of multiple repositories. Most companies adopting this structure will have one master repository that links to the other project repositories.

Why Are More Companies Choosing Monorepo?

Mono repo is straightforward compared to other organisational structures we'll look at in this segment. However, there are plenty of reasons companies opt to use this type of structure. When developing software and managing products in a modern fashion, consistency is essential to keep things running smoothly and ensure everything is accomplished correctly. Collecting all your code in one location allows for maximum consistency. If developers know that they will always work with the same code, they are more likely to stay consistent in their practices. This consistency ensures that all projects are developed and managed similarly. Additionally, Monorepo can be beneficial if your company has multiple teams working on various projects.

Significant Benefits of Using a Monorepo

There are plenty of benefits to using a monorepo, but these are some of the most notable ones.

New features roll out across multiple projects: you can instantly roll out new features across various projects. This is particularly useful if you have multiple projects or products that rely heavily on each other. For example, if you have a project that tracks sales and a project that tracks customer support, they may both be using the same code or database. If you have one of those projects go down, the others are likely to be affected as well. Having your projects in one location allows you to roll out new features across all projects easily.

Less expensive Code bases: This is significantly less expensive to implement and much easier to manage than having multiple code bases. Willingly, it's easier to see how your development team performs. When everything is housed in one location, it becomes much easier to see your company's performance. This is particularly helpful if you have multiple teams working on various projects. In addition, it's more accessible to onboard new developers. Since everything is in one location, it's much easier for new developers to get up to speed and start contributing. They can spend less time looking for information and figuring out where everything is.

Easier collaboration: When your teams can access each other's code from a single location, it becomes much easier to collaborate. You can quickly jump from one project to another without worrying about where the other team members' code is stored.

Organisational consistency: If your teams use the same code, they must adhere to the same standards. This can help boost consistency across your entire development, making it easier for your teams to work together. It's easier to see how your business is performing. Suppose you're trying to understand how your company is performing. In that case, tracking within the confines of individual code bases can be challenging. When everything is in one location, it's significantly easier to see how your company is doing.

One version of everything: Leveraging Monorepos means no more worrying about incompatibilities because your projects depend on conflicting versions of third-party libraries.

Easier Atomic commits: Generally, in the Monorepo environments, atomic commits across projects are much simpler and more manageable as everything works together on every commit. So, there are no groundbreaking changes when you fix everything in the same commit.

Developer mobility: You can consistently build and test applications written with different tools and technologies. As a result, developers can confidently contribute to other teams' applications and make sure their changes are safe.

Things to Be Aware of When Using a Monorepo

There are some things to be aware of when it comes to Monorepos. However, they don't outweigh the benefits outlined above. To adopt this organisational structure of your code repositories, you must make significant changes to how you work. You'll likely have to retrain your team so that they know how to work within this new system. You will need to make significant changes to your development process to ensure everything runs smoothly. It's important to remember that all organisational structure version control systems are perfect for some companies. It will help to keep your team's needs and abilities in mind when considering new organisational structures.

Organisational Efficiency

Organisational efficiency is one of the biggest reasons companies turn to Monorepos. Organisational efficiency refers to how well your team can use its resources and complete their work. When your team operates at peak efficiency, they can do more in less time with fewer resources. Organisational efficiency is a two-way street – not only do your employees need to be operating efficiently, but you also need to provide them with the resources they need to do their jobs. When it comes to the resources that your employees need, one of the biggest things is consistency. When you have everything in one place, it's easier for your team members to know where everything is and what they can use. This consistency helps to ensure that everyone is using the same resources, which makes it easier for them to work together.

Disadvantages of Monorepos

There are a few disadvantages to using a monorepo. However, they are minor compared to the benefits outlined above. As with any organisational structure of source code, there are also some disadvantages. If you adopt Monorepo, you must ensure that your team knows the potential consequences. Developers may need clarification if they need to get used to working with Monorepo. Sometimes confusion can be damaging if the team has already been working together and is already familiar with their process. If one team member suddenly needs help understanding how to commit, it can cause problems and slow everyone down. Especially if the teams are cross-functional – if one team member is doing two or three different jobs, they likely won't notice that they're confused.

Some Considerations of Code Culture and Quality

When your code lives in one place, it's easier to track how it's progressing and ensure that it's being developed according to your standards and expectations. When your code is in a monorepo, you must have strict rules about code additions and contributions. Otherwise, your code base will likely become cluttered and difficult to navigate. This clutter can be detrimental to the health of your code. It can make finding the code you need more challenging and make it more likely that people will make mistakes when contributing to a project. When your code is in one place, enforcing these rules and ensuring everything is up to your standards is easier.

In a Nutshell, using a monorepo can be beneficial for several reasons. The biggest reason is that it makes it easier to collaborate between teams. If you have multiple teams working on numerous projects, collecting their code bases in one location can help you to collaborate more easily. It also makes it easier to track how your business is performing. If you have all your code in one place, it can be easier to see how your business is doing.

CHAPTER 2: MODERNISE APPLICATION ARCHITECTURE

Microservice: A Software development architectural and strategic approach in which software is decomposed into small and independent services that communicate thru APIs.

Time and again, the software has proven its value by enabling the efficient execution of business processes. The software helps by breaking down work into smaller, discrete tasks to be performed by smaller components of software called services. These software services are known as microservices. These software programs are designed to perform a single task or set of related functions to operate independently. This chapter will overview microservices and how you can leverage them in your organisation. This chapter will also cover general pros and cons before adopting microservices, along with use cases. Tried to cover examples from real-world companies that have implemented microservices successfully. This chapter will provide an overview of Microservice architecture.

What is a Microservice?

A microservice is a software component designed to perform a single task or set of related functions to operate independently. The main difference between a microservice and a traditional software application is that microservices are more lightweight and are designed to run in a distributed environment. In addition, with minimal coordination, microservices can run in isolation, making them scalable and replaceable. Typically, a microservice can run in a single process or a small set of processes that one or more hosts manage. However, a microservice will likely depend on other microservices to complete its work.

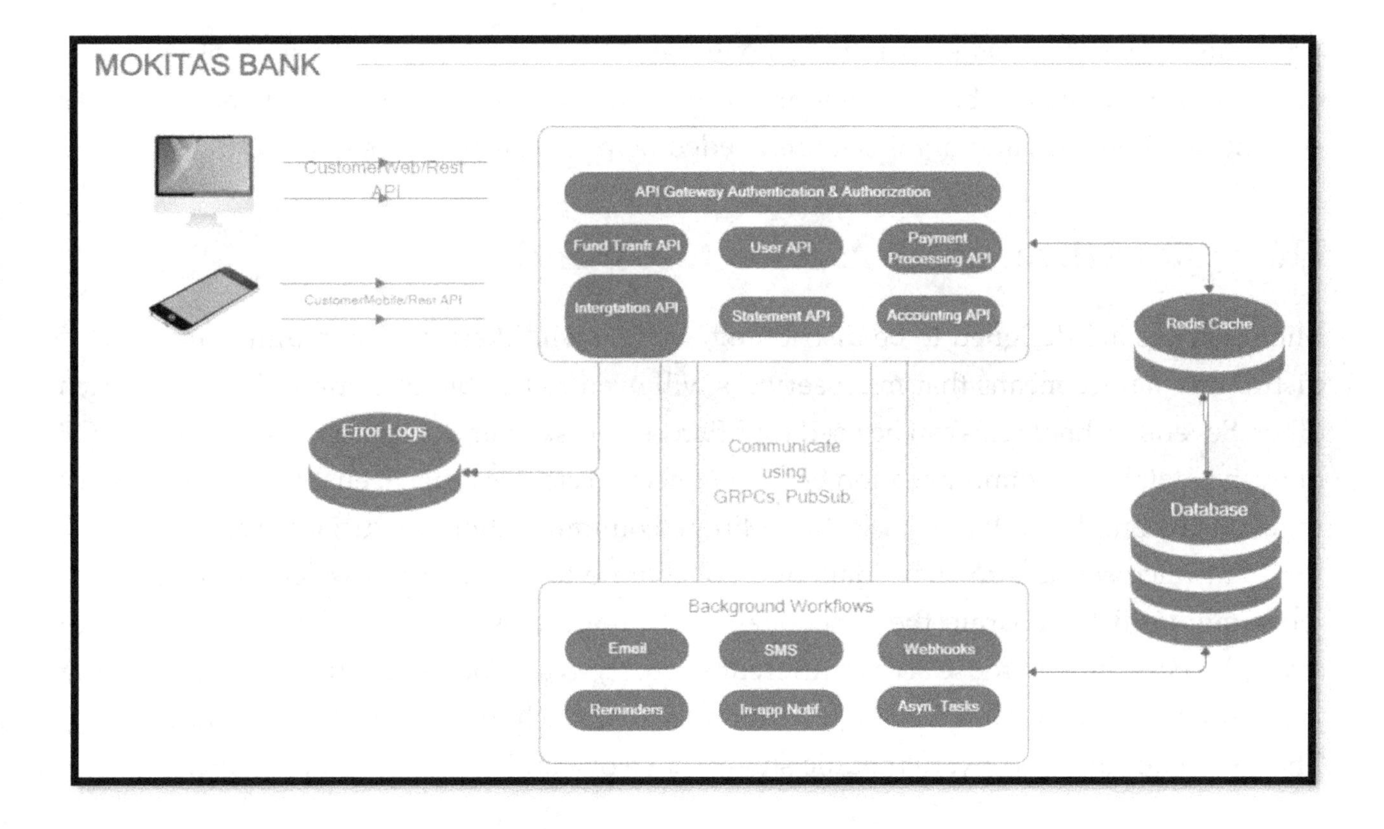

Why the shift to Microservices?

The shift to microservices is not without its own set of challenges. Many who have attempted to adopt the architecture have failed. The reason is that while the architecture is very sound, it requires a different way of thinking. You must break down your monolith into smaller services to achieve the desired outcome. The adoption of microservices results from organisations moving away from the traditional software architecture known as service-oriented architecture (SOA).

The main reason for this shift is to remove the difficulties experienced with SOA. These difficulties were mainly because the architecture needed to design to meet the business's current requirements, and organisations needed help to scale their systems.

How does Microservice Architecture work?

Microservices are designed to be distributed, so they will likely run-on multiple hosts. This distributed nature means that microservices will need to be able to communicate with each other. Several technologies can be used for Microservices communication, such as HTTP, TCP, or even a database. Communication between microservices is critical, enabling them to work together to complete a larger task. In addition, communication is crucial because it allows different microservices to share data and collaborate to perform a task. Decoupling is the technique used to separate the functionality of one microservice and break it down into smaller pieces that can reuse across different microservices. The key to successful decoupling is ensuring you stay within the Single Responsibility Principle (SRP) of software engineering. The SRP states that a software module should have one and only one responsibility.

Key characteristics of a microservice

A microservice architecture has many characteristics that set it apart from monolithic architecture. The following factors are unique to microservices and can leverage to create a highly scalable and robust architecture.

Modularity: Each microservice should be developed to perform one objective. This modular behaviour will enable Microservices to be more independent and communicate with one another more easily.

Scalability: Each microservice should be able to be scaled independently. This attribute enables the architecture to be scalable and handle the changing loads on the system more efficiently.

Fault Tolerance: Each microservice should be designed with fault tolerance in mind. This characteristic will enable the system to be more fault-tolerant and ensure that it can keep running even when a microservice has failed.

Key Benefits of Microservices

Business agility: When you move to a microservice architecture, each microservice is designed to be independent and can upgrade or replace without affecting the rest of the application. It makes it easier to respond to change and improves business agility.

High scalability: Microservice can be scaled to suit its requirements. This nature of the microservice will enable the architecture to be mounted more quickly and can do it at a granular level.

Easier to develop: It is easier to develop microservices than a monolithic system. Because of the nature of microservice, it can develop independently and in parallel.

More straightforward to implement: Teams can launch standalone applications using a microservices architecture without disrupting other services in the design. This capability enables developers to add new modules without restructuring the entire system. In addition, with a microservices design, businesses can easily add new functionality.

Differences between Monolith vs Microservices Architecture

Architecture: A microservice architecture is very different from a monolithic architecture. A monolith will be a single large application. At the same time, a microservice architecture will be a collection of small, independent applications that can be scaled and managed independently.

Deployment: Deployment of a monolithic application will differ from a microservice architecture. The entire application can deploy as a single unit in a monolithic architecture.

However, in a microservices architecture, each microservice will deploy individually and likely run on a different host.

Scaling: A monolithic application's scaling differs from microservice architectures. In a monolithic architecture, you scale the entire application. However, it is easy to scale each microservice independently in a microservice architecture.

Communication: The communication between the components in a monolithic architecture differs from that of a microservice architecture. In a monolithic architecture, there will be a single-entry point into the application. One service will be responsible for communication. In the Microservices ecosystems, every microservice will have to communicate with the others in a microservice architecture.

Defining Microservices

Each microservice will handle a particular part of the business functionality; the microservices must clearly define what the service does. Therefore, the first step in determining a microservice is understanding its purpose. You can do this by analysing the existing application and identifying the functionality that is being used the most.

The next step is to decide on the granularity of the functionality is broken down into smaller services. This granularity can vary from extensive functionality to small functionality. It is crucial to remember that each functionality you break down into a microservice should have the same business value. The next step is to decide on the name of the microservice. It is recommended that you choose a name that is easy to understand and describes the functionality for which the microservice is responsible.

Disadvantages of Microservices

While many advantages and benefits are discussed in the earlier part of this chapter, it's worth reading about the disadvantages. If any environment with microservices is not appropriately implemented, that will create chaos. With that in mind, this section will discuss some disadvantages of moving to a microservice architecture. We should carefully consider these factors before moving to a microservice architecture.

Hard to Manage: Moving to microservices will likely result in many services that need to manage. These behaviours of Microservice can make working on the architecture more difficult and time-consuming, given the increased number of services.

Harder to Test: With many services, it will be harder to test each individually. This attribute will make it very hard to maintain and robustly test the system.

Microservices have higher setup costs: Although cloud-based microservices have financial benefits, such as long-term cost savings, there are initial deployment costs. An organisation needs a solid hosting infrastructure with support for security and maintenance. Even more crucially, it will require qualified staff to oversee all services.

When to use Microservices?

You must assess several factors to decide if microservices are the right design for your business. These factors include your existing architecture, scalability, fault tolerance, and the level of communication between the various modules in your application. For example, you can use microservices if your architecture still needs service-oriented architecture. And if there is a significant level of communication between the modules in your application. But on the other hand, microservices are a good solution if your application still needs to meet service-oriented architecture requirements. And if you want to create a highly scalable and robust application.

This concludes our overview of microservices. However, suppose you are in the process of adopting microservices. In that case, I hope that this chapter will help you understand what they are and entail.

CHAPTER 3: APPLY CLOUD ENGINEERING

Cloud Engineering: An engineering discipline is applied to cloud computing through cloud engineering. The commercialisation, standardisation, and control of cloud computing applications are handled methodically.

DevOps is an approach to software engineering that aims to align software developers with other team members by breaking down traditional organisational barriers between disciplines. In a DevOps environment, programmers and others collaborate more closely from the beginning of a project or product development. Hence, everyone understands their peers' challenges and can help them find solutions. The cloud has opened new ways for organisations to implement DevOps philosophies and techniques. The benefits of cloud DevOps are numerous: greater agility, faster time to market, lower costs, and improved collaboration among team members. In addition, cloud services remove many implementation challenges of on-premises software. Let's look at how cloud computing and the DevOps approach can help your organisation adopt a more collaborative culture while speeding up deployment times and reducing expenses. This chapter will help to open your eyes to Cloud Computing and the DevOps Approach: What Is Cloud DevOps? How Cloud Engineering helps DevOps transformation

What Is Cloud DevOps?

Cloud DevOps is an approach to software delivery that aligns software engineering with other disciplines through continuous integration and deployment. In a cloud DevOps environment, cloud-based tools, and platforms, such as containers and serverless computing, automate gathering software code from multiple sources and deploying it into production.

The increased automation reduces the time it takes to build, test, and deploy new software. In a traditional software development process, separate teams handle testing, quality assurance, and programming operations. In a cloud DevOps environment, these teams work together from the beginning of a project, so everyone understands their peers' challenges.

Common Cloud computing services

It can take time to keep track of all the different cloud computing services and solutions available. There are so many acronyms, after all! It's easy to get lost in the details. PaaS, IaaS, SaaS What does that even mean? Do you need to know any of these things to be a successful IT professional? Well, yes and no. Knowing about cloud services is optional for DevOps Transformation. However, it can help you advance your DevOps Transformation journey by learning more about how technology is used today in the DevOps transformation phase. Especially in startups. Keep reading for a brief breakdown of each of these three main types of cloud services: Infrastructure as a Service (IaaS), software as a Service (SaaS) and Platform as a Service (S). It will help you to understand the different types of cloud operational models.

What is Infrastructure as a Service?

IaaS is a cloud service that provides the hardware resources to host virtual machines, virtualised networks, and other virtualised services. In simpler terms, IaaS provides the infrastructure on which other services can run, which includes storage, network resources, security features and even utilities like power and cooling. If you host your business's servers in a public cloud, you're likely using IaaS. IaaS is sometimes called "infrastructure as a utility" because the infrastructure is used as a raw resource that anyone can tap into. This infrastructure is owned by the service provider and maintained by them. IaaS users pay for the help they use and nothing more. With IaaS, it is easy to scale up or down as needed.

What is Software as a Service?

In a nutshell, SaaS is software that is hosted and maintained by the provider. This means that you can install it on your end users' computers or pay to maintain it. All you need to do is log into the service provider's website and use the software there. The provider takes care of the rest, including security and maintenance. Small businesses, enterprises and individuals most commonly use SaaS. Software as a service is often used as an alternative to on-premises software. With this model, you don't have to invest in expensive, long-term licensing agreements. Instead, you pay a subscription fee, which may be on a monthly or annual basis. In addition, you can tailor SaaS offerings to businesses of all sizes. You can find software for almost any industry, regardless of your company's size.

What is Platform as a Service?

Platform as a service, or PaaS, allows developers to create applications without worrying about managing infrastructure. PaaS providers handle operating systems, databases, security, networking, and other everyday IT tasks. You write the software and host it within the provider's platform. PaaS is often used for creating web and mobile applications. PaaS is often referred to as "application as a service," The two terms are usually used interchangeably. The main difference between PaaS and IaaS is that with PaaS, you don't have to worry about the underlying infrastructure. Instead, PaaS providers take care of the infrastructure and let you focus on the apps.

Cloud-Based Automation and Continuous Integration

Cloud-based automation and continuous integration help you build and deploy software more quickly. Automation is essential for DevOps transformation, helping you remove human error from the development process. CI is the automated process of testing and building software while considering code commits and team collaboration. In a DevOps environment, CI processes are configured to run parallel to reduce the time required to test and build a new application. You can test code integrations, permissions, and security with cloud-based CI. You can also check the quality of software products before they hit the market, so your users can experience fewer issues and defects. In a DevOps environment, CI processes run in the cloud and are accessible from anywhere.

Parallel Running of Tests in the Cloud

Cloud-based testing tools help you run parallel tests across many different devices and browsers, eliminating the need for in-house testing on devices. Parallel running lets you complete test cycles much faster when you test across multiple devices and browsers. Quality assurance teams that use parallel running to try across multiple devices can see a significant reduction in test cycles and cycle times. QA teams can test across mobile, virtual, and hardware devices and browsers when they use cloud-based parallel running. This will eliminate the need for hardware and local testing environments, helping cut costs. In addition, parallel running lets you quickly scale up or down your test cycles to match your needs and demand.

Cloud-Based Collaboration and Communication

Collaboration and communication are essential parts of any successful DevOps transformation. Cloud-based tools let engineering teams access and share information with stakeholders and other team members. Collaboration helps team members stay in sync with one another, removing the need to communicate via email or other less efficient channels. Cloud tools can also help you communicate with customers and other stakeholders, such as marketing teams when they request information. Cloud-based communication tools, such as team collaboration software, can help you improve organisational workflows.

Better Decision-Making Through Real-time Data

Real-time data insights help engineering teams make better code and product deployment decisions. With cloud-based data analytics tools, you can view data insights in real time without downloading and installing software. Real-time data insights help you optimise your organisation's workflow and make better product management decisions based on current data. In addition, real-time data insights help engineering teams make better code and product deployment decisions. For example, you can view data insights about customer usage and adoption to understand better how your software is being used. This information helps you make more informed decisions about product enhancements, code revisions, and other considerations.

The benefits of Cloud-based DevOps

Cloud-based DevOps and software engineering practices help organisations achieve the following goals:

Faster time to market: Cloud-based tools and platforms allow you to build and deploy new software quickly. You can get the latest software to market faster and respond more rapidly to customer needs.

Reduced costs: Cloud-based tools help avoid needing in-house testing environments and hardware. Cost reduction is a quick win if anyone is looking to reduce the costs associated with purchasing and maintaining expensive hardware.

Greater agility: Collaboration and communication tools help engineering teams stay in sync with one another and stakeholders. Real-time data insights help you make better decisions, ensuring you are making product enhancements and other choices based on accurate data.

DevOps in the Cloud improve productivity.

Cloud-based DevOps helps engineering teams achieve greater productivity by automating many manual processes that slow down team members. Automating manual processes allows engineering teams to focus on other tasks, helping them finish more quickly. In addition, cloud-based tools and platforms can integrate with existing software, allowing you to use the tools you already have. This will enable you to implement many of the practices of cloud DevOps without a significant investment in new tools.

In a Nutshell, Cloud computing services are often categorised based on three main types: IaaS, SaaS, and PaaS. IaaS provides the infrastructure for software, SaaS provides software for end users, and PaaS delivers the platform for developers to build software. These are just three of the many types of cloud services. There are many others to choose from, including colocation, managed services, hybrid and B2B services. Regardless of your cloud service, always keep an eye on security. This way, you can ensure that your data is safe and secure.

CHAPTER 4: LOW CODE PLATFORM A NEW WAY

Low code platform: Provides a graphical user interface (GUI) development environment for creating application software.

I'm starting this chapter with some questions. Low code platform? How does a Low-code platform help DevOps? Is it needed? Continue your questioning. This chapter will help you to elucidate all your questions.

Before climbing into the tree, let us take the first step. Low-code development integrates the best of both globes in a single platform where non-technical users and professional developers can apply their skill sets. In addition, this new breed of development approach will ease collaboration and co-develop solutions. Low-code development allows users of all skill levels to collaborate on software applications without sacrificing the benefits of professional developers. Furthermore, businesses can develop customised applications more effectively than ever by combining low-code, no-code, and high-code systems. This chapter explains low-code development, how it works, and why it benefits any organisation.

What is Low-Code Development?

Low-code development is a software development methodology in which users can create custom applications without writing code. Low-code systems can take a wide range of input, including structured data, unstructured data, business rules, user requirements, etc. Then, these systems generate a fully integrated software application on top of a single code base, regardless of the input source. In other words, low-code development is creating custom software applications by piecing together pre-written code modules — without writing any code. It's an alternative to traditional development cycles, where fully-customised applications can build from scratch without reusable code. Businesses increasingly rely on software for critical tasks like customer service, sales, procurement, etc. The low-code development helps organisations quickly create custom software with minimal effort.

How Does Low-Code Development Work?

You can start with a blank slate when you create a new application using low-code development. You can import data from existing systems or start with a high-level design and let the system walk you through the details. You can also use visual tools to sketch out your application or create a predefined app such as an enterprise or SaaS app. Using these tools, and you will first decide what your application will do. For example, you might add some information about the users interacting with the app. You might also choose how the app will get data from other internal systems and talk to parties outside your organisation. Then, the system will translate your high-level ideas into a finished application that real people can use.

How Does Low-Code Platform help DevOps Transformation?

Low-code platforms are great tools for DevOps teams. They allow you to build and deploy software quickly and easily. Low-code platforms can reduce the time it takes to write new code by as much as 90%. They also make it easier to test and debug apps.

With all this in mind, choosing the right low-code platform for your team is essential. There's no one-size-fits-all solution. You'll need to consider the size of your development team, the complexity of your application, and the speed at which you want to build software.

You can use Low-code platforms in several ways. Some allow you to build code directly on the web or in an app. Others let you create new apps by connecting other services. If you want to go full-stack with your DevOps approach, a low-code platform might fit your fit.

Benefits of Low-Code Development

Low-code development has many benefits, including reduced costs, improved collaboration, and better security. Organisations that use low-code development systems can expect to reduce costs because they don't have to hire as many developers to build custom software from scratch. This is because low-code development uses reusable code modules that have been proven in production, which reduces time to market and minimises the risk of bugs and security issues. Low-code development also improves collaboration, enabling non-technical users to create custom software applications without sacrificing the benefits of professional developers. In addition, users who can create products that meet their organisation's needs are less likely to rely on outside vendors and suppliers. This can make it easier to enforce internal policies and create a more controlled environment.

Downsides of Low-code development

Although low-code development can produce high-quality, scalable software applications, it also has disadvantages. One of the most significant issues with low-code development is that it produces similar results to no-code development.

The difference between no-code and low-code is mainly in marketing. A no-code platform focuses on the creation of no-code apps. It will try to guide users through the app creation process. In addition, A low-code platform allows users to make changes to the existing code. Low-code platforms are great for creating variations of an application or making changes to an existing application. However, they could be better for creating a new app from scratch. Low-code development systems are also susceptible to security breaches, primarily if not appropriately managed. To combat this issue, organisations should use a single-source code platform that allows developers to see and alter all aspects of the code base. This approach will allow them to patch any vulnerabilities they discover while also allowing them to add new features to the platform.

Low code platforms are software development platforms that automate parts of the software development process. They allow developers to create and test software in a short amount of time by automating repetitive tasks such as data collection and data validation. As a result, DevOps teams use low-code platforms to build and deploy applications faster than they could. These platforms can also help teams collaborate more efficiently by reducing the need for frequent updates and rework.

Low-code platforms have many benefits, but they can also present some challenges. A low-code platform needs to be well-designed to avoid causing more problems than it solves. Low-code platforms must be easy to use and maintain so everyone can get the most out of them.

Which Platform Should You Use?

Many low-code and no-code development platforms are available, each with strengths and weaknesses. If you're starting, research the top low-code development platforms to get a feel for what's available. Once you know what each platform offers, you can determine which is best for your organisation. Some top low-code development platforms include Microsoft Azure, Appian, Automation Anywhere, CloudCraze, iLogic, and UiPath. Before you decide which platform to use, you should understand the problems each solves, the ideal users, and the potential drawbacks.

Microsoft Azure is a cloud platform that allows businesses to easily create web and mobile apps that integrate with other services. The platform is powered by artificial intelligence and machine learning to deliver real-time insights. Apps built on Azure can be accessed from any device and come with built-in security and compliance.

Appian is a low-code platform specialising in business process automation, analytics, and data visualisations. It's designed for large organisations that need to automate their most complex business processes. Depending on your needs, you can either create apps from scratch or modify existing apps with zero code.

Automation Anywhere is a business process automation platform that allows users to create apps that run on PCs and mobile devices. This platform is built for scalability, so it can quickly adapt to your changing business needs. It also integrates with various third-party tools, including other low-code development platforms.

CloudCraze is a SaaS platform that enables users to create, customise, and deploy apps without having any technical experience. The platform is designed for marketers, salespeople, and anyone who needs to create custom software.

iLogic is an enterprise-grade low-code development platform that allows users to build and deploy custom apps on any device or operating system. It's designed for businesses of any size and can integrate with other systems. Finally,

UiPath is an enterprise automation platform that uses drag-and-drop functionality to create automated workflows, web apps, and more. This platform integrates with almost every major business application and can access from any device.

Why Low-Code Development Is Beneficial

As you can see, low-code development offers many benefits for organisations of all sizes. Most notably, it makes it easier for non-technical users to create customised software applications. Also, Low-code platforms are beneficial in companies where non-technical staff are responsible for creating custom apps without having any coding skills. Low-code development allows these employees to easily create the software they need without relying on technical staff. The nature of the Low-Code platforms can save your organisation money and increase employee productivity. Low-code development also allows organisations to develop new products quickly and with fewer resources. You can create a new product with low-code development in weeks or even days rather than months. Low-Code platforms make it easier to respond to recent market trends and create new products that meet your customers' needs.

In a Nutshell, now that you understand low-code development, how it works, and why it's beneficial, you're ready to create your first app. To do so, you'll first need to choose the best low-code development platform for your organisation. Once you've decided on a platform, you can use it to create your application. Once your app is up and running, you'll want to ensure its well-maintained and scalable. To do so, you may need to ensure you have the right engineering skills in-house. Then, you'll like to schedule regular code reviews and audits to identify issues early on.

CHAPTER 5: DEVELOPER EXPERIENCE

Developer experience: Describes how a developer generally feels and perceives a technical product.

DevOps is the collaboration between software developers and other IT professionals so they can streamline processes and get products to market faster. Improving the experience for both teams is essential for DevOps success. A recent survey found that DevOps teams prioritise creating a great developer experience over any other work element. So, we know what you're thinking: how do you improve the experience for developers and operators? What needs to change, who needs to change it, and how can we make that happen? Creating an Ultimate Developer Experience (DEX) handbook for your team is the answer. This document will be a collaborative resource for your organisation and empower each team to elevate their game.

What is an Ultimate Developer Experience

For any organisation to ensure efficiency, quality, and the retention of competent technical personnel, developer experience is crucial. Unfortunately, the developer experience often needs to improve when businesses grow more prominent, technologically savvy, and broaden their tech stacks. This increase could overwhelm developers, which would be detrimental to their output. As a result, companies have begun appointing teams tasked with upholding strict DevEx requirements to resolve this problem.

The development speed depends on how well-versed the developer is in the DevOps procedures and tools that are available to them as developers, and there are hundreds of them. Some people may find the DevOps set of practices frightening. A developer will only be as successful or satisfied if they feel overpowered by them. The developer's expertise is crucial in this situation. Companies should actively consider giving developers everything they require in a single, streamlined location so they can concentrate on what matters.

DEX Defined

DEX or DX stands for "developer experience," a term that grew in popularity as businesses began shifting towards DevOps. The idea behind DX is that companies should design their systems and processes around those who use them. When you create a great developer experience, you create an environment where developers feel empowered, supported, and able to do their best work. Achieving DX is an ongoing process that requires constant attention. It's tempting to focus on getting new features to market quickly and overlook other elements of the work—but remember, your development process includes more than just code. All the tasks that go into creating a product, such as testing, debugging and even deployment, are part of the developer experience.

Create a Culture of Collaboration

To create a great developer experience, you'll have to foster a culture of collaboration within your organisation. Collaboration doesn't just mean people are talking to each other; it means working together to achieve a shared goal. You'll also want to ensure it's easy for your developers to get the information they need from one another. Organisational tools like Slack, Zoom and JIRA are essential for building strong developer relationships and cultivating a collaborative culture. Your team's workflows should account for different types of collaboration. Some processes will require tight collaboration, while others may require more independence. For example, you may have one team responsible for creating a new feature. In contrast, another team tests it out, and another team sets it live. Even if these teams all work together, more communication may be needed than with the test team.

Create an Environment for Learning and Growth

Even if your developers love what they do, they may want to try new things to spark curiosity and self-growth. When designing the developer experience, remember that your team members may want to take advantage of new skills or technologies. Create a room for collaborative learning with whiteboards and computers that can use for online courses. You could also create a mentorship program where senior developers are paired with junior developers and allowed to share their knowledge. Learning opportunities can be more than just technical skills, too. You can create an environment for personal growth by encouraging your team to take advantage of mental health resources, participate in open-source initiatives and make time for self-improvement. Your team members should know they are supported in their efforts to learn and grow.

Help Developers Learn, Grow and Thrive?

The best way to support your developers is to ask what they need to succeed instead of designing your workflows and tools with an assumption of what's best for the team. Instead, strive for transparency and encourage everyone to share their suggestions for improvement. You can do this by implementing the following practices:

Have a suggestion board or medium for ideas: Set up peer mentorship or a lunch-and-learn program

Hold regular retrospectives: Include user experience as a core metric.

Help Operators be Proactive and Responsive

Operations teams are responsible for ensuring the tools used by developers are reliable and functional, as well as communicating with other groups to troubleshoot issues. They're also responsible for keeping the rest of the organisation apprised of the status of projects. While some of these tasks may be part of the development process, how they are handled can make a big difference in the developer experience.

Your ops teams can improve their workflows by:

1. Automating as much as possible
2. Integrating with other systems
3. Getting involved in development discussions
4. Noticing when communication channels are being neglected

How to Design a Good Developer Experience in Your Workspace

These are general guidelines for designing a workspace that supports and enhances the developer experience.

Collaboration: Make space for collaboration and ensure quiet space for uninterrupted work.

Tech: Keep your tools up to date and ensure they're easy to access.

Environment: Make sure your space supports the type of work your team does.

Ergonomics: Be mindful of your team's health and well-being. - Light: Natural light is best for mood and productivity.

Privacy: Make sure each team member has a designated place to work. –

Productivity: Remember the basics, like having a calendar and tracking the progress of tasks.

Retrospectives: Make time to reflect on what's working and what could be improved.

Repurposing: If your space needs to be fixed, repurpose it.

Safety: Make sure hazards are removed, and toxic areas are avoided.

Consistency: When your team members know what to expect, it helps them do their best work.

Short Developer Feedback Loops to Enhance Workflow

One of the key elements to enhancing workflow is creating short feedback loops. Feedback loops are the moments in a workflow where you stop and check how things are going. They can help you adjust along the way to catch everything necessary. There are lots of different types of feedback loops you can use to make your workflow more efficient. Here are a few worth considering for your team:

Check-ins: These are one-on-one meetings where you check in with each team member about their work.

Retrospectives: These are group meetings where you talk about how the last cycle of work went and what can be improved.

Project or Sprint reviews: These are when you bring stakeholders into your workspace and show them the project's current state.

Checklists: These are lists of things that you need to do.

What Problems Dx Can Solve

Greater collaboration, better communication and efficient workflows are the hallmarks of a successful DevOps transformation. They're also the building blocks of a great developer experience. You may also notice other side benefits, such as reduced stress, better health, and stronger relationships.

Suppose you've implemented all these elements of good developer experience. In that case, you should be well on your way to seeing a difference in your product. DX can help you reach better product outcomes by providing the perfect environment for your team to work in and be more productive. It also allows you to understand your team members better and make changes to support them and their workflow. This can also help you avoid getting overloaded and stressed out because you have everything under control and understand what needs to be done.

In a Nutshell, the goal of DevOps is to create a more efficient workflow. However, you need to consider the developer experience to achieve your objectives. By creating an Ultimate Developer Experience, you can establish best practices for your team and achieve the goals of DevOps. Collaboration, better communication, efficient work

Thank you

CPSIA information can be obtained
at www.ICGtesting.com
Printed in the USA
BVHW020043231222
654897BV00011B/207